Pavel Kudlak

PAVEL KUDLAK:
A Screenplay

Mehmet S. Tekbaş

White Crane Books (Canada)
Windsor, Ontario

Published by White Crane Books (Canada)

White Crane Books' publications may be purchased online at: www.amazon.com and www.amazon.co.uk.

For information please contact: whitecranebooks@live.com

Copyright © 2012 by Mehmet S. Tekbaş
All rights reserved including the right of reproduction in whole or in part in any form.

Library and Archives Canada Cataloguing in Publication

Tekbaş, Mehmet S., 1953-
      Pavel Kudlak : a screenplay / Mehmet S. Tekbaş.

ISBN 978-0-9879706-1-9

      I. Title.

PS8639.E395P38 2012   C812'.6   C2012-905532-8

Disclaimer: Pavel Kudlak is an original work of fiction. Any similarities to real events, people, places, and/or names are merely coincidental.

Photo by Canadian Arts Productions

Printed in the United States of America.

*Dedicated to my mother, Ayten
and to my late father, Ahmet*

FADE IN:

BEGIN FLASHBACK:

EXT. DRIVEWAY – DAY – 20 YEARS AGO

A typical neighborhood in suburbia U.S.A. It's early morning. The streets are virtually deserted. Nothing of consequence is happening. The birds are CHIRPING and the sun is shimmering splendidly.

Suddenly, Jimi Hendrix fills the SOUNDTRACK with "ALL ALONG THE WATCHTOWER."

The sun saturates the screen. Gradually, a powder blue Mustang comes into focus—parked in the driveway of a two-storey Colonial near the end of a cul-de-sac. A white cargo van sits idling behind the Mustang, partially jutting out onto the street. Bit by bit, we dolly toward the van... the vehicle appears to be empty but we can't be sure—its windows have been altered with aftermarket tint. We stall our movement and slowly pull back.

As the music of Jimi fades in the background, we hear VOICES from inside the house. Clearly, a man and a woman are having a fiery argument. We push closer.

Pavel Kudlak

INT. FAMILY ROOM – DAY

Now on the main floor of the house. A dapper dandy, sporting an untrimmed goatee, SHOUTS insults at a CRYING white WOMAN. We move back and forth during the exchange—unable to determine the nature of the fight. It's obvious that the MAN is enjoying himself. The Woman, on the other hand, is on the verge of a physical collapse.

They look to be about the same age. She is probably a little younger—in her late-twenties—with a dancer's grace and rhythm, having a distinct foreign accent. His ungainly movements and manner indicating a rougher origin.

                    MAN
          You're unfit to be a wife!

                    WOMAN
          Please… it doesn't have to be this
          way.

                    MAN
          Be quiet! Enough of you.

                    WOMAN
          Try to understand my side. We've
          been married six years.

Pavel Kudlak

>MAN
>Bitch, you don't know a goddamn thing!

Soon... we realize that these two lovebirds should never have tied the knot.

Then... the Man becomes angrier and more violent. He is angrier than Mike Tyson ever was—if that is possible. He pummels the defenseless Woman with his arms and legs.

She lets out a blood-curdling, hellish SCREAM and runs to escape from his madness. The Man viciously tackles her to the floor... he straddles her chest... slaps her face... and begins to tear off her clothing. The Woman gamely fights back... palming and clawing at his face.

>WOMAN
>Please, no. My baby!

>MAN
>Now I'm gonna fuck you, bitch!

The Woman's cry for mercy only serves to relish his cruelty.

> WOMAN
> (desperately)
> I'm begging, please don't hurt me.
> No! No, you're hurting me.

The assault is in full swing. Fists, elbows, teeth, and knees rain down on the unlucky woman.

INT. BEDROOM – DAY

We're inside the bedroom of a little boy, on the second floor of the house. A plush teddy bear sits on a bedspread of dinosaurs. A toy railroad track cuts across the floor of the room and several toy cars are also nearby.

The door of the closet is ajar. We hear the heart wrenching SOBS of a terrified child.

We follow the sniffles...

INT. BEDROOM CLOSET – DAY

Inside the small dark room, among the many petite shirts and pants, hides a SMALL BOY, he is nearly four years old. His young face is soaking wet—he has been crying and hiding for a while.

We hear the brutal ASSAULT on his mother. The Small Boy desperately tries to stifle his sobs; he's trembling with fear.

Then... All is quiet.

> SMALL BOY
> (waterworks drying a little)
> Mama! Mommy!

Clearly, the house is empty except for the young lad whimpering in the closet.

INT. FAMILY ROOM – DAY (LATER)

The main floor resembles Baghdad after the American bombing. Every lampshade and piece of furniture and everything else is either broken or toppled over.

The partially nude, lifeless body of the Woman lies on its back—she's been strangled. Her head and torso slumps to one side, with her eyes and mouth wide open—indicating that she fought her rapist to the end.

END FLASHBACK.

Pavel Kudlak

The screen is black for a moment.

Over black we hear the CRASH of a cue ball striking the other balls.

CREDIT SEQUENCE:

PAVEL KUDLAK

As the OPENING CREDITS play we study Pavel's cue stick handling skills.

INT. POOL HALL – DAY

A pool parlor reminiscent of the 1920s. It's exactly 10:00 in the A.M. Several tables are under red Naugahyde. The room isn't yet crowded. A KID in baggy blue jeans sweeps the floor. The sign over the snack bar declares, "Johnny Shotz cares about your game."

PAVEL KUDLAK, a fit white dude with flowing jet-black hair, barely 25, is practicing on a full size table. He's wearing a pristine white suit— demonstrating perfect grace, control and skill.

We watch him play a straightforward double into the middle... and witness the cue ball easily coming into position to pot the blue into the same.

Pavel Kudlak

THE FOX behind the counter throws him a glance. The shapely redhead definitely is eye-candy for the boys. Soon, she brings Pavel a steaming hot cup of coffee... sets the porcelain down on a side table, smiles broadly and splits.

Pavel takes a sip... chalks up a beat—not in any hurry to decide on his next shot. Several fellas take notice and come closer to watch the maestro play.

After a beat... Pavel pots a red. Then he RIFLES the black into the near corner pocket. The cue ball drops on a red midway between the pink and black spots to give him an angle into the opposite corner. Pavel launches the red into the corner, followed by the pink.

He chalks and stands back to ponder his next series of shots.

Then... he SINGS a red into an end pocket. The cue ball gets nice shape on the blue into the middle.

The Kid runs over to spot the blue.

END CREDITS.

Pavel Kudlak

Pavel lines up another shot. The pool hall is dead silent, you can hear a pin drop… THEN…

> JAKE (O.S.)
> (barely audible)
> I can beat his ass!

> PAVEL
> (looks up)
> 'Scuse me. That's fuckin rude, man.

Pavel lays his cue on the pool table as he throws a glance at a black dude leaning on a stool—the 24-year-old pool hustler known as JAKE.

Jake glides toward Pavel wearing a grin.

> THE FOX
> (to Jake)
> Hey, you leave him alone or I'll call the manager.

> PAVEL
> (to The Fox)
> Be cool, sweet pea.

JAKE
(sticks his hand out)
I'm Jake… that's my mother's
choice of name, not mine. She
named me after the badass
motherfucker, Jake LaMotta.

Pavel and Jake shake hands.

PAVEL
(mocking disbelief)
No way!

JAKE
Matter of fact, my little brother's
name is Ali. Another brother is
Rocky.

Pavel looks at him, smiles—he cannot believe his ears.

PAVEL
No shit!
(beat)
Jake, don't take this wrong. But…
I mean, what kind of a person
names her precious boys after
some fuckin boxer. No matter how
great they are, you just don't do it.

Jake throws him a look.

> JAKE
> Anything else bothering you?

> PAVEL
> No... But if you're asking, I'm curious—can you at least take care of business?

> JAKE
> You mean can I fight. Can't lick my black lips... I'd rather lick Puerto Rican pussy.

> PAVEL
> That's funny. I understand.

Obviously, Jake doesn't think it's funny nor does he understand.

> JAKE
> My mom loved to watch people beat the crap out of each other. Now she is gone... died last year on the Ohio Turnpike, coming to my dad's funeral.

A grim pause.

Pavel Kudlak

          PAVEL
Damn, that is a fuckin shame.
    (beat)
They were separated?

Jake leans on a pool table nearby, his energy has left his body—he can barely move his head to indicate yes or no.

Pavel looks at him... then, surveying the table.

          PAVEL
Black in the end.

He sends the black into the corner pocket... the object ball rolls to get perfect shape on a red. Pavel chalks...

The Kid rushes to spot the black... then he dances away from the table doing a backstroke— imitating the late Michael Jackson.

Next... Pavel plays a power shot. He HITS the cue ball hard, sending it round the table off four cushions. Jake smiles—as does everyone else that is watching.

Power shots look great but no professional player will attempt them if there is a choice because the opportunity for things to go wrong is too great.

JAKE
This nigger will make you curse
dumb ass shots like that—

PAVEL
(interrupts)
Stop right there, Jake. The fuckin
trash from your mouth ain't worth
sayin yes to... besides... I can
clean your clock but I don't wanna.

JAKE
So you got principles, is that it?

Pavel chalks while analyzing his options on the pool table—ignoring the remark. With the object ball tight on the cushion, Pavel shoots the ball by using right-hand side. He misses a shot for the first time.

The cue ball flies off the pool table and CRASHES loudly onto the hardwood floor... rolling toward the vending machine. The Kid quickly dashes after the object ball and snags it just as it is about to roll under the dispenser.

Pavel and Jake smile.

The Kid wipes the ball on his clean white shirt and places it on Pavel's table.

Pavel has had enough—he jams his cue stick into the wall rack. Evidently, he has been playing with a one-piece house cue.

> PAVEL
> See you around, Jake.

Pavel walks out of the pool hall.

Jake waves farewell behind him.

> THE FOX
> (to Jake)
> Creep!

DISSOLVE TO:

INT. THEATER AUDITORIUM – DAY

The theater is vacant except for Pavel sitting in the front row. He's in black jeans and a white cotton shirt with the sleeves rolled up—looking like a critic.

CHARMIAN is on stage. Then... CLEOPATRA (played by LARA), IRAS and ALEXAS enter the stage. Everyone is dressed in period costume.

Clearly, the actors are rehearsing Shakespeare's ANTONY AND CLEOPATRA.

          CLEOPATRA
Where is he?

          CHARMIAN
I did not see him since.

          CLEOPATRA
See where he is, who's with him, what he does: I did not send you: if you find him sad, say I am dancing; if in mirth, report that I am sudden sick. Quick, and return.

Alexas goes.

          CHARMIAN
Madam, methinks, if you did not love him dearly, you do not hold the method to enforce the like from him.

          CLEOPATRA
What should I do, I do not?

          CHARMIAN
In each thing, give him way, cross him in nothing.

CLEOPATRA
Thou teachest like a fool: the way
to lose him.

CHARMIAN
Tempt him not so too far; iwis, for
bear: in time, we hate that which
we often fear.

After a momentary pause.

Pavel stands and APPLAUDS with enthusiasm.

PAVEL
Bravo! Bravo! Bravo!

The actors smile and bow graciously toward Pavel. He's still on his feet, into it.

CLEOPATRA
(to Pavel)
Thank you, thank you. You are
very kind, sir.
(beat)
Baby, I'll be down in two shakes of
a puppy's tail. Sit comfortably.

Cleopatra rushes off the stage.

Pavel sits comfortably, sipping his cola and watching the actors rehearse.

The director gives pointers to the actors. We don't hear them. They continue rehearsing as a stagehand removes props.

INT. LIVING ROOM (PAVEL'S APT.) – NIGHT

Pavel and Lara stroll into a spacious Spartan pad carrying groceries and wine. Pavel leads the way. The most conspicuous items decorating Pavel's dig are a worn-out leather couch and a wooden desk with a keyboard and monitor. The apartment is plainly that of a young trendy intellectual. Various scholarly books and papers are scattered everywhere. In one corner of the room sits an aquarium filled with black and white Choubi goldfish. Numerous exotic plants and bonsai finish the ensemble.

Finally, we get a chance to check out Lara, the significant other—a buxom, twenty-something Hollywood-type dish. She shows off black Spandex slacks with revealing Spanish style shoulder-less blouse, showcasing a spider tattoo on her left shoulder. The underside of the spider's black abdomen has red markings, in the shape of an hourglass, indicating that it is indeed a black widow. Lara is definitely a babe with the goods and the wherewithal to match—and she lets you know it.

Pavel drops the groceries on the floor and waltzes over to Tinkey, a short hair blue mackerel tabby, lounging on the dining table. Pavel strokes Tinkey's fur, the cat PURRS... lies on her back— enjoying the attention. Pavel rubs her tummy.

> PAVEL
> Tinkey, bad girl. Dinner tables aren't for lazy cats to lounge on. Did you miss daddy?
> (beat)
> C'mon Tinkey, be a good girl and jump off the table. Daddy got you a treat!

Then... Pavel gingerly picks up the cat and sets her on the floor. She HEARS interesting sounds coming from the kitchen and sprints in that direction. We follow along.

INT. KITCHEN (PAVEL'S APT.) – NIGHT

We come upon a fully equipped, crisp white kitchen. Black countertops, white cabinets— nothing like what we would expect from a young male. The groceries and wine sit on the marble countertop. A large wok sits nearby.

Lara is CHOPPING carrots on the face of a wooden block. She's not paying any attention to Pavel or Tinkey. Garlic cloves, yellow onions, lemon grass, red chili peppers, and mushrooms sit on the countertop awaiting consumption.

Tinkey is in the kitchen—now in scouting mode. Then... she affectionately rubs herself against Lara's leg.

ROCK MUSIC coming from the living room.

> LARA
> (loudly)
> Your majesty, what would you like me to prepare? I can make a new Vietnamese dish I learned from Jake. Or, how about chicken with lemon grass and cashew nuts? And—

Pavel Kudlak

Pavel now stands in the kitchen behind Lara... feeling her up.

PAVEL
(interrupts)
Mm mm. Sounds yummy! I heard my name, so...

Lara's chop chop has slowed down considerably.

LARA
(playfully)
Hey, stop what you're doing right now... we're supposed to be cookin dinner.

Pavel just continues exploring Lara's body... then... he moves to southern hemispheres, his right hand resting firmly on Lara's butt. Eventually, the other hand joins the fun.

PAVEL
Exactly. And I wanna help. Did you know that I'm a dicing master? I can chop and dice your carrots quicker than you can say Ming dynasty.

Lara pulls away from Pavel's grasp—unsure of what to make of him.

LARA
(playing along)
Ming dynasty!

PAVEL
Hey, not so fast, I'm serious. I love to chop and dice... Don't you think that's strange?

Lara grabs a handful of mushrooms from a tub and begins to expertly quarter each one on the block. Not taking him serious.

LARA
Not really, if you think about it. Lotta people like to chop things, especially onions; it seems to relax them. I knew a fellow who loved to iron in his spare time. I know it is not the same as chopping onions but it's almost the same. He was definitely weird.

PAVEL
Care to explain?

Lara expertly quartering mushrooms. Pavel waits.

LARA
Well, he would set up shop in front of his TV with a good long movie, so he didn't have to keep flipping channels. And he'd have a stack of grilled cheese sandwiches in front of him—along with a pitcher of iced tea—'cause he didn't wanna keep running to the kitchen. And he would stand there for several hours, like an automaton and iron shirts all day.

PAVEL
Oh yeah, that's nothing. I think and fantasize about chopping and dicing every day. It's a part of my being.
    (beat)
I may have been a dangerous Japanese samurai in a past life.

LARA
    (teasingly)
Maybe you were just a harmless Japanese peasant that had to do a lot of chopping!

At that, both break out laughing. A beat.

Suddenly... Pavel grabs a shiny cleaver from the countertop and holds it up high like a Ninja assassin from feudal Japan, ready to cut down an enemy.

Lara immediately steps back to give him room. SWOOSH—Pavel cuts through the air. Lara is completely taken by surprise—she's speechless.

Pavel gets into it.

> PAVEL
> Did you know the word "assassin" comes from the Arabic word, "hashshashin," which means hashish eaters?
> (then)
> Do you wanna know why? Because the assassins drugged themselves with hash before killing someone.

Pavel tosses the cleaver onto the counter.

Lara quickly snatches the object into a bottom drawer and places it under a bunch of other items—just to be on the safe side.

Pavel Kudlak

LARA
No, I didn't know that. Thanks for sharing that information with me. I think I've just peed in my pants. Nevertheless, thank you for putting down the big knife—

Pavel pulls her into him.

PAVEL
(interrupts)
Don't be such a scaredy cat.

He gently bites Lara's ear lobe… continues biting. She resists his overture.

LARA
(excitedly)
I have a surprise for you—coconut cream pie and "Breathless."

Almost instantly, Pavel stops all sexual play activity. Now there's some distance between their bodies.

PAVEL
I know where this is going I'm not stupid. The first part I'm crazy for. But what's Breathless? It's not porno, is it?

LARA
Of course not, silly.

Lara lobs several diced chicken pieces into the hot wok... gives a shake.

PAVEL
(realizing)
Not another fuckin classic film. I thought we agreed I didn't have to watch 'em anymore.

LARA
I know I made you watch bad ones before and I am truly sorry for that. But, sweet cups, you will adore this, I promise. It's Jean-Luc Godard's best work.

Lara turns over the browned chicken nuggets... tossing in the chopped onions... as Pavel chucks sliced carrots into the mixture—popping one into his mouth for good measure.

PAVEL
The last time we did this you were happily snoring before the credits ended.

Lara tosses several garlic cloves into her masterpiece.

                    LARA
         I do not snore, you liar!

                   PAVEL
         With hell you don't. I have the
         entire episode on tape. Videotapes
         do not lie, Lara.

Pavel grabs a handful of cashew nuts and places several into his mouth... he flings the others into the SIZZLING wok.

                    LARA
         On tape? You do not!

INT. LIVING ROOM (PAVEL'S APT.) – NIGHT (LATER)

Chopsticks, dirty dishes and leftover food sit on eight-sided plates on the coffee table. A half-eaten coconut cream pie lies on a dessert plate nearby.

Lara is SNORING away on the couch next to Pavel—looking like she missed most of the movie. Pavel is wide-awake watching television.

On TV: Patricia informs the police of her lover's crime in the film, BREATHLESS.

A momentary pause.

Pavel sits at the dining table writing feverishly on a sheet of yellow notepaper. A marijuana joint burns in an ashtray. Tinkey, the mischievous tabby, is again lounging on the dining table.

The DVD plays in the background as Pavel continues to write. Then, abruptly, he tears up his work and chucks it into the full wastebasket.

EXT. CEMETERY – DAY – (DREAM)

A solemn MINISTER wearing a burial cape performs last rites at an open grave.

>   MINISTER
> Rest eternal grant unto them, O Lord, and may light perpetual shine upon them.

The Minister makes the sign of the cross. Several men and women are crying.

Then... the casket is lowered into the ground.

Pavel Kudlak

The Minister bows his head as two men FILL the grave with earth.

> MINISTER (O.S.)
> Naked came I from my mother's womb and naked shall I return. The Lord gave, and the Lord hath taken away; blessed be the name of the Lord, Amen.

The Minister makes the sign of the cross and moves away.

A Small Boy, about four years old, stands on top of the freshly covered grave, sobbing quietly. He wants to say something but the words won't come out.

> SMALL BOY
> Mama!

An ELDERLY WOMAN bends over the young lad, TALKING softly to him. A scarf covers her head.

> ELDERLY WOMAN
> Go-ahead sweetheart say whatever you want. It's all right.
> (pause)
> Go-ahead baby. Speak to your mother.

Pavel Kudlak

INT. BEDROOM (PAVEL'S APT.) – NIGHT

Pavel and Lara are sprawled on a sleigh bed. Lara is barely dressed in Pavel's wrinkled white shirt. Pavel is in moonlight blue pajama bottoms with T-Rex plastered all over.

Almost as soon as we cut to Pavel, he wakes from his sleep, as if chased by Lucifer. He is drenched in sweat.

PAVEL

Mama!

Pavel's start wakes up Lara.

LARA

Baby, what's wrong?

She wipes Pavel's forehead with her hand.

PAVEL

She called for me.

Lara strokes his chest. Concerned.

LARA

Shh, shh… you've been dreaming.

Coming to his senses.

Pavel Kudlak

PAVEL
I can't explain it but something is wrong.

He has this eerie look in his eyes.

LARA
Pavel, your mother is fine. Lately, you've been thinking more about her—and that's perfectly understandable.

PAVEL
Don't patronize me, Lara.
(hesitatingly)
Maybe you're right. I've been under enormous stress—

LARA
(interrupts)
Shh... I'm sure wherever she is, she's well.

She kisses his chest and face.

LARA
(continuing)
Honey, I had no idea you missed her so much.

After a beat… they embrace… then, Lara kicks it up a notch. She's all over him—nibbling and kissing his chest, shoulders and abdomen. Clearly, the woman is horny. Pavel is unresponsive. He acts as if he needs a case of Viagra in order to play in the sand box. For once, Lara's sexual tinkering does not crank his motor.

> PAVEL
> Would you mind if we took tonight off?

Lara's movements suddenly go into slow-mo and finally cease altogether.

> LARA
> Of course not. Why should I mind? If you can stand it for one lousy night, so can I—

> PAVEL
> (interrupts)
> It's not a competition, Lara.

Lara studying him.

> LARA
> You're in one of your moods again, aren't you?

Pavel Kudlak

PAVEL
I ain't in any of my fuckin moods!
And I ain't gonna make excuses.
And I don't wanna explain a
goddamn thing.

Pavel and Lara stretch out on the bed; both stare up at the blank ceiling. After what seems like forever, but only a few moments—Lara jumps off the bed, moves to Pavel's CD player and thumbs through a stack of CDs.

Pavel on the bed, looking at her.

The speakers BLAST out Patsy Cline, singing, "I FALL TO PIECES." Lara dances around the room... shaking her ass in rhythm.

LARA
C'mon dance with me, lazybones.

Lara loosens several pearls of her white shirt... while she jiggles her sexy version of the twist. Her rhythmic gyrations keep on rolling... then the song ends and so does Lara's little dance.

Pavel looks up at her, smiles.

THEN... without warning... Lara does a grand flying leap—landing plain on top of Pavel.

Pavel Kudlak

Their big bed collapses with a loud KABOOM.

They look at each other for a moment. Pavel brushing away errant hair from her face.

PAVEL
You broke my bed!

She just looks at him. Then they kiss... Lara straddling him, legs wide apart, as Pavel's hands do a detailed exploration of her body.

LARA
Please suck my breast.

Pavel's mouth obeys the order, locking tightly onto her raised nipple.

LARA
(continuing)
Don't ignore the other one she gets jealous.

Pavel hungrily kisses her other breast... Lara looks at him... holding his head encouragingly.

LARA
(continuing)
Is it to your satisfaction, my lord?

PAVEL

Uh-huh.

Pavel continues kissing both breasts... then... his head moves between Lara's legs... he lingers at that zone patiently... Lara lays her head back, eyes closed... kneading her breast.

EXT. STREET IN SUBURBIA – DAY

Pavel is at the door of a house talking with a young housewife holding a toddler. We don't hear their conversation. A moment later, Pavel turns and walks away.

He walks to the next house. An elderly woman, MRS. HENSLEY, opens the door. She looks at him weird.

PAVEL
Hello, sorry to bother you, I'm Pavel Kudlak—

MRS. HENSLEY
(interrupts)
Is it really you, Pavel. My gosh— look at you, how you have grown.

She touches Pavel's arm.

Pavel Kudlak

> PAVEL
> You know me?

> MRS. HENSLEY
> You lived in that house.
>> (points to a house across the street)
> You'd ride your scooter everyday—up and down the sidewalk, in front of our house.

INT. HENSLEY HOUSE – DAY

Pavel and Mrs. Hensley sit across from each other in the living room.

> MRS. HENSLEY
> My Ernie passed away four years ago and all our children have grown and moved away. They were much older than you.

She holds out a framed photograph of her children.

Pavel gives a polite glance.

> MRS. HENSLEY
> (continuing)
> I've always wondered what became of you... Ernie thought you'd be an architect like your father—

> PAVEL
> (interrupts)
> Mrs. Hensley... do you remember the day my mother died?

> MRS. HENSLEY
> I remember that day vividly—there were all kinds of police and ambulance people in the neighborhood. They asked all kinds of questions. We were just coming home—Ernie and I... we saw them putting your father into a police car... it's so sad, how is your father?

Pavel just looks at her.

> MRS. HENSLEY
> (continuing)
> We were visiting his sick mother that morning—she died several weeks later—pancreatic cancer. We couldn't believe it… it's so sad. They loved each other—always holding hands.

> PAVEL
> Anything unusual happen that day?

> MRS. HENSLEY
> (shakes her head)
> Nothing that I can recall. There were rumors about a van—but that was just a rumor. I'm sorry I'm unable to help.

Pavel gets up to leave.

> MRS. HENSLEY
> (continuing)
> Please come again, Pavel.

> PAVEL
> Thank you, I will.

Mrs. Hensley gives him a big hug, then she kisses him on the cheek.

> MRS. HENSLEY
> (suddenly)
> There is one thing that has bothered me for years—your mother always received flowers but she always threw them out—I'd see the unopened box on the sidewalk from my kitchen window. I teased Ernie mercilessly—wanting him to send me flowers, but he never did. It probably means nothing. Just thought I'd mention it… I told the police.

DISSOLVE TO:

INT. 12-STALL BARN – DAY

A well lit modern farm stable. All the trunks and harness bags are open. Several standardbreds, sturdy and wide-bodied, are standing in crossties in the shed row.

SPUNKY and his three CARETAKERS (#1, #2 and #3), work quickly. The clock on the wall indicates 9:55. By this time, the racehorses have trained and exercised—now much of the activity centers on putting them away.

Pavel Kudlak

Spunky, the trainer, is an imposing former biker with a mass of tangled hair and a beard that comes up to his wild bloodshot eyes. He resembles Blackbeard the pirate, but lacks his temperament. Spunky weighs 217 pounds exactly. We don't know how he got into racing horses.

The Caretakers are just that: working grunts. All are waiting for that break to becoming trainers themselves some day.

Caretaker #3 is giving an equine athlete a soapy bath in the wash stall.

Other caretakers are engaged in packing feet, rubbing horses, filling water buckets, or cleaning tack. They move from one task to another without any urging—they know what to do.

Spunky puts a beautiful chestnut colt in the crossties. Then he goes into a tack trunk, grabs some antiseptic wipes and cleans his hands. Next, he selects a medication vial from the trunk and cleans the top of the vial with an alcohol swab. Then... we see Spunky attach an uncapped needle into a syringe and insert the needle into the top of the medication vial as he holds the vial upside down, gently TAPPING its side as the syringe fills. Finally, Spunky removes the needle from the medication bottle and expels extra medication and air from the syringe.

Caretaker #1 working nearby.

> SPUNKY
> (to Caretaker #1)
> Gimme a hand.

Caretaker #1 takes the chestnut colt out of the crossties and holds his head. The colt is a bit unsteady.

> CARETAKER #1
> (to horse)
> Whoa…

Spunky wipes a small area of the colt's neck with alcohol wipes, finds his vein and injects the medication.

> SPUNKY
> In about an hour this horse will feel like a rock star. Bute works fast. Put Elvis in a paddock by himself and let him relax.

The groom puts the chestnut back in the crossties.

Pavel Kudlak

Spunky notices a bay mare shifting her feet in the crossties. He walks over to the mare and bends down to check her front shins—running his hand on the back of her legs.

>   SPUNKY
>   (to Caretaker #2)
>   Tub her right away… there's some
>   swelling and heat.

Caretaker #2 takes the mare to the wash stall, puts her in crossties and gently places her front legs inside a large water tub. The mare is not thrilled about having her feet inside a plastic tub. Eventually she agrees to stay put. The groom fills the tub with cold running water, attaching the hose to the tub with a large clamp. The water runs freely out of the tub. Then he grabs a cooler off the rack, tosses it on the mare and clamps it at the breast.

Spunky is on a cell phone—and moving his hands all over the place like an Italian barber. We don't hear him.

Pavel Kudlak

EXT. PADDOCK – DAY

Inside the fenced paddock, some hay and a water bucket sit under a tree in the shade. The doped up chestnut is running around like a champion racehorse. He looks and feels as fit as a fiddle, thanks to the miracle of modern pharmaceuticals.

INT. PICK-UP TRUCK – DAY – MOVING

We're traveling in a red pick-up on a scenic country road. Pastures, paddocks and four-board oak fences line the route.

ANGELO FEDELE (a.k.a. JAWS) is doing the driving. He looks to be about 50 years old. A lit cigar hangs loosely from his mouth.

His trusty equine trainer, MIKE LAKE, sits in the passenger seat. He is much slimmer than Jaws and not yet forty. However, he's been around some and is not afraid to speak his mind. Both men are dressed like wannabe cowboys: boots, Western shirts, blue jeans, and cowboy hats.

Mike cracks his window open.

> MIKE LAKE
> I thought you wanted to quit.

JAWS
I changed my mind—I enjoy it too
much. Open the window.

Jaws scanning the landscape, trying to read road signs that hurry by. Mike studies him.

MIKE LAKE
In my opinion, he's asking too
much for the fuckin horse. The
colt has had only two wins, a lousy
maiden and a non-winner of two up
in Canada—

JAWS
(interrupts)
However, it's how he won 'em.
He was up by ten lengths in his last
and five in the previous. Mike, I
don't have to tell you how
impressed I tend to be about that
sort of thing.

Jaws throws his cigar into the ashtray.

MIKE LAKE
I just think we should be a little
cautious with this dude, given his
reputation and background and all.

Pavel Kudlak

The pick-up slows down and turns into the lane of a farm. We see majestic apple trees line both sides of the laneway. Then we pass through the wooden gates of the facility... and see a large two-storey farmhouse. Several horses are grazing and relaxing in paddocks nearby... a closed-cab John Deere kicks up dust and stones as it pulls a track harrow over the surface of the farm track.

> JAWS
> That's fine. I pay you to have an opinion... Look him over real good, will you do that for me, Mike. The vet will take care of the rest.
> (then)
> Please, mind your P's and Q's. I want this fuckin colt.

Jaws parks the truck in front of the barn. We see several jog carts and race bikes leaning against the building. A sign on the structure reads, "Green Apple Racing Stable." The two men walk inside.

INT. 12-STALL BARN – DAY (LATER)

Spunky's facility. Now, much of the work is finished. The horses have been put away. The caretakers are finishing up by either cleaning tack, rolling brace bandages or sweeping the walkway. The tempo is much subdued.

Spunky walks toward the men.

>   SPUNKY
>   (to the visitors)
>   Hello! Glad you came… I was
>   worried you would miss the turn.
>   I've done it myself several times—
>   ended up in Kalamazoo.
>   (extends his hand to Jaws)
>   How in the hell are you?
>
>   JAWS
>   (shakes his hand)
>   Ah, I complain all the time but
>   nobody listens. Mike will tell ya,
>   he's been with me—
>
>   MIKE LAKE
>   (interrupts)
>   We raced against each other in
>   New York, Angelo. I never forget
>   a worthy rival.

                    SPUNKY
               (laughs)
          Likewise. Those were good times.
               (then)
          The colt is in the paddock. We
          should go see.

They exit the barn. We tag along.

EXT. PADDOCK – DAY

The chestnut colt is relaxing in the paddock; he definitely enjoys running free and chasing imaginary mares. The men stand at the oak fence, estimating the colt.

                    JAWS
          Damn, he's a looker. Such grace
          and speed.

Jaws throws a glance in Mike's direction.

                    SPUNKY
          Mister Fedele, this colt can go
          back-to-back quarters in 26 flat.

Jaws and Mike exchange looks.

> JAWS
> No doubt. The problem I have is
> this: he took a long time getting to
> the races. What's up with that?

> SPUNKY
> Absolutely nothin to worry about.
> Had a little issue with shins, just
> like all horses. We wanted to make
> sure he was 100 percent before we
> raced him.

Suddenly, Mike picks up a small rock and throws it in the direction of the colt. The spooked colt bolts like lighting.

The men grin.

> JAWS
> What do you think, Mike? Do you
> want him in your barn?

> MIKE LAKE
> Fuck ya, who wouldn't.

> JAWS
> (to Spunky)
> I'm leaning toward 500 cash and
> that's my final offer—

Spunky throws him a glance.

>   SPUNKY
>   (interrupts)
> In that case, I'll have my people
> draw up papers and I'll ship 'im to
> your barn tomorrow, after your vet
> looks him over.

>   JAWS
> I'll courier a certified check.

After a beat... everybody shakes hands, everybody is happy.

>   MIKE LAKE
> Then it's settled.

>   SPUNKY
>   (to Mike)
> I'll throw in his harness and race
> bike.

We see Jaws and Mike Lake walk to their truck as Spunky enters his barn.

The men drive off the farm.

Pavel Kudlak

INT. "TEEZERS" NIGHT CLUB – NIGHT

We're inside a sleazy strip club just off Main Street. The place is humming with all kinds of people. Latin rock BLARES in the background.

Two flirtatious Latin-American girls are on stage stripping, doing their version of the modern cha-cha-cha. A sign with a figure of a stripper towers behind the stage. The orange letters of the neon reads, "TEEZERS."

A sexy nude Mexican girl is dancing inside a mock prisoner's cage—it's about twelve feet off the floor.

Pavel and Jake are sitting near the stage, sipping cold drinks and sharing laughs with a couple of hot dancers. Both are dressed to impress. Pavel is in an old bomber jacket over faded blue jeans while Jake wears black slacks with a yellow silk shirt and tie. He has a dark-skinned honey sitting on his lap, trying to make a meal of his ear lobe.

Pavel notices Spunky approaching their table from the bar.

>   JAKE
> Why don't you lovely ladies take a hike?

The lovely ladies murmur as they take a hike.

Pavel stands to greet Spunky.

                  PAVEL
Hey, Spunky, good to see ya sport.

The old buddies shake hands and hug each other.

                  SPUNKY
Same.

                  PAVEL
         (playfully)
You still waterin the drinks?

The men sit.

                  SPUNKY
         (nods to Jake, grins)
No man, my wife made me give
that up. You would not know
about things like that. Single guys
have it made! Forget about me,
how in the heck have ya been? I
haven't seen you in ages. Are you
still playin the ponies?

Spunky playfully SLAPS Pavel's shoulder and almost knocks him to the floor.

SPUNKY
(continuing)
What brings you to the good part of the city?

PAVEL
I'm glad you brought that up, Spunky. 'Cause the truth is, my gambling buddy and I are experiencing cash flow problems.

SPUNKY
Is that all? Fuck dude, why didn't you say so. See me before you split—I'll fashion one just for you.

Pavel and Jake exchange glances.

PAVEL
Spunky, you're a fine human being. A true Christian and a believer in God, justice and equality.

JAKE
I completely agree. A fine human being.

SPUNKY
(grins)
Do not be lickin me just yet.
Recall the last time we tried this
maneuver the fuckin driver
dropped his whip in mid-stretch.
Everybody wants to kill him but
me, 'cause I was busy fucking his
wife that night.

Pavel throws him a glance.

PAVEL
I'll be damned, you sly dog. You
didn't lose any money and you got
laid. For your information, I cried
for seven days on account of that
fool.

Jake shakes his head, trying not to laugh too hard.

SPUNKY
(laughs)
Some gangsters make money and
kill... I choose to make money and
live. I'm in it because I'm too
dumb for anything else. Can you
see me as a schoolteacher? But
never mind that—

A fistfight has started between two Mexicans. They throw a couple punches at each other but nothing lands. Suddenly, both fighters pull out their shiny switchblades. They are threatening to cut each other to little strips of flesh... then one of the men jumps on the bar and attempts to do a Chuck Norris imitation to his friend's head— missing completely, of course.

Spunky notices the commotion and gets up.

>   SPUNKY
>   (continuing)
>   Don't stay a stranger, come by the
>   farm and say hello to the kids.
>   (beat)
>   I'll send over some drinks.

Spunky walks off toward the bar.

>   PAVEL
>   Jake, lemme take care of some
>   business and we'll scoot outta here.

Pavel heads toward the rear of the strip club. The sign on the door reads, "Do Not Enter." Pavel enters.

After a beat... The two Mexican fighters are now sitting together at the bar, drinking—old friends again.

The girls come back to the table and take their seats.

>JAKE
>I think I've developed a cramp in my leg, would you ladies massage it for me!

The girls giggle knowingly. Jake is now out of his chair and shaking his leg to help the circulation along.

Then he grabs the girl seated nearest, who incidentally happens to have the biggest tits, pulls her to his body and plants a life-size juicy kiss on her red Mexican lips. She squeals.

>JAKE
>(continuing)
>Ladies, it's been a gas!

Jake throws some money on the table.
Pavel and Jake exit the club.

FADE TO:

EXT. BARN "D" (RACETRACK) – DAY

We're at a Standardbred racetrack outside the barn of Mike Lake. There's a big letter "D" on the building.

A pick-up truck and horse trailer are parked near the sliding doors of the barn. The trailer's gate is open and the ramp is down. Mike Lake and JACK are on the trailer. The men are off-loading a chestnut colt. Jack is standing at the horse's head—guiding him off.

Jack is a gritty old black fellow who's been around the backstretch all his life. He has a drinking and gambling problem and he has had both for as long as he can remember but he knows everything that there is to know about racehorses, gambling, and drinking.

>   JACK
> C'mon boy. Let's get you inside.

The colt appears to be in severe distress; he can barely walk on his own.

Jack studies him.

JACK
(continuing)
Mike, this colt is in fuckin pain. I suspect he's lame with chronic sore shins.

MIKE LAKE
I was thinkin the same, Jack… I'm in deep shit. Jaws paid a pretty bunch for him and I OK'd it.

The men lead the troubled colt into the barn.

INT. BARN "D" (RACETRACK) – DAY

All tack trunks, harness bags, and coolers are painted blue with gold trimming. Clearly, this is Mike Lake's racing stable—his name appears on almost everything.

Jack puts the colt in crossties.

Mike bends down and exams his shins. The colt is not too crazy about having his sore shins touched by anyone.

Jack watches… then takes a good long swig from his flask.

Two grooms walk over to give a look-over to the new member. We can't make out what they're saying. The colt is fidgety and restless.

Mike is pissed.

> MIKE LAKE
> Jack, don't give him anything for pain or otherwise. We can't contaminate the blood. Make him comfortable and put him away. I'll deal with this.

Jack looks him over real good, from top to bottom.

> JACK
> He's quite muscular, Mike. And feisty. I can understand how you were swayed. He may come back in nine months.

> MIKE LAKE
> Jack, I was duped. Jaws will never race him in conditioned company.

Mike stomps to the tack room.

> JACK
> (to the grooms)
> The show is over, fellas.

Jack fills a coffee can with feed... and throws it all into the colt's tub.

The caretakers go back to their chores... Jack leads the chestnut into his stall... and takes his bridle off. The animal dives into his feed tub.

INT. TACK ROOM (BARN "D") – DAY

Mike slumps in an old wooden armchair—he looks dog-tired.

Old programs, a computer monitor, and a telephone rest on the desk. Numerous bridles and bits hang on hooks on a wall. Additionally, there is a cot and a first-aid kit in the room, nothing else.

He picks up the telephone and punches in numbers. Then...

> MIKE LAKE
> (into phone)
> Hi, doc. It's Lake. I need you to
> do some urgent blood work for me.
> (beat)
> I suspect he was doped. We have a
> couple hours before the drugs leave
> his system entirely.
> (pause)
> I'll be here.

Mike hangs up the phone and exits the tack room.

DISSOLVE TO:

EXT. DRIVEWAY (BUNGALOW) – NIGHT

The patio lights are on. A secluded bungalow. An old, mint condition green Jaguar sits in the rear driveway, the trunk lid is raised—the nose pointing to the road.

We see two white dudes transferring shoebox-shaped plastic bags of something from the backdoor of the house into the trunk of the vehicle. The men work quickly to fill the baggage compartment, making sure that everything is neat and tidy.

Pavel Kudlak

CLOSE ON THE BAGS OF MARIJUANA
Neatly packed into the trunk. The trunk cannot hold anything more.

They SLAM the trunk and walk into the house.

We HEAR the car alarm being set. A moment later, the patio lights go dark.

INT. "JAGUAR" – NIGHT – MOVING

A green Jag dodges traffic in Chinatown. In the front seat are Pavel and Jake. Pavel is behind the wheel, driving as if he is in some driver's education class for high school kids.

C.U. of the steering wheel. The speedometer NEEDLE locked on the digit "30."

> PAVEL
> So, as I was saying—when I was a young lad back home in South Bend, Indiana, I 'yooz to wonder at the mystery of the world. Know what I mean, Jake?

> JAKE
> Sort of. Mind if I burn one?

Pavel Kudlak

PAVEL
Be my guest, but please do not
burn my fuckin leather.

Jake pulls out a fancy cigarette case, spreads his weed on some rolling paper and rolls it into a perfectly shaped joint. Next, he takes out an antique Zippo lighter from a pocket and lights his smoke, then SNAPS the Zippo shut.

JAKE
Then what happened?

Pavel gathers himself.

PAVEL
As I'm saying—I would be
thinkin… why in hell are the fucks-
in-power keeping us all in the
dark? I mean, I had a sense of the
truth… I knew.

Jake takes a toke from the weed and passes on the joint to Pavel.

Pavel accepts a short, polite hit. Then he points it back to Jake.

PAVEL
(continuing)
I mean I had strong feelings—a clear sense that the world was a nasty secretive place and that God had fucked up. I was a little kid, but I knew that most stiffs were stupid and did not know damn about anything.

Jake is busy toking on the weed—hardly listening to him.

The Jaguar stops at a red light. A grandmother strolls across the intersection, pushing a baby carriage.

JAKE
Man, I understand perfectly. Kids don't know a bloody thing… at least you were able to guess that much.

Pavel throws him a glance.

PAVEL
Suppose so. However, there is a bit more to this chatter than just that.

JAKE
(a puzzled look)
How so… But before you continue with your philosophical inquiry into the lack of meaning of your life, I want you to take a good hard toke.

Jake hands him the half-smoked pot.

PAVEL
Thank you.

Pavel just holds the joint.

JAKE
(seriously)
Kudlak, I want you to understand something. This ain't any motherfuckin ordinary, garden-variety dope. This, friend, is my personal high-grade mixture. Grown organically by my grandmother, Bess. She brought back the seeds from Holland personally.

Pavel inhales deeply from grandma's pot.

                    JAKE
              (continuing)
        It's guaranteed to enlighten
        prophets and fools like us.

At that pronouncement, Pavel draws in another monster toke. After a beat... the Jaguar comes to a full stop in the middle of the intersection. The mind altering effects of grandmother's concoction has hit home.

                    PAVEL
              (a stoned look)
        I'll be... damned!

As if following a script, both men open their windows simultaneously and stick their necks outside the car... gulping fresh air.

                    JAKE
        Phew, that is so much better.

Before long... both necks are back in the car and the windows are up again.

Pavel punches the gas pedal.

Pavel Kudlak

> PAVEL
> As I was sayin… now I realize that this world isn't secretive after all. Because it bares itself all the time, if we only let it… potentially, we can know everything.

> JAKE
> Yeah man, I know exactly what you're getting at. Reading fat library books can make one smarter than a ghetto pimp.

Pavel tosses the joint into the sedan's ashtray—barely containing himself.

> PAVEL
> Wrong, wrong, wrong. That is not what I'm espousing. If you recall, I said something about no hiddens. That means there are no secrets and no secret agenda.

Jake has begun to get the drift. A state of pure annoyance settles over him.

JAKE
Just hold on a minute, Socrates.
We can go into this in depth if you
wanna, but that is not necessary.
Because you mister, have lost your
religion.
(beat)
You have become a disbeliever.

They are sitting at a traffic light and the light has turned green. Pavel's hands are off the steering wheel—one hand rests on the back of Jake's seat, the other is in his lap.

PAVEL
So you don't agree.

Jake doesn't reply. After a moment... the traffic sitting behind the two men are HONKING loudly at them.

JAKE
The light is green.

That's all it takes. Pavel's window zips down and his entire torso is hanging out the window—he's SHOUTING obscenities at the other vehicles.

Then he's back in the car and they ROAR out of the intersection as the light turns red.

PAVEL
Let me get this right. You think
we will never completely know
this world because some things
will always remain hidden to
people.

JAKE
Yes, I'll go along with that, for the
moment.

Jake throws a glance at him, not sure, where this is going.

The gathering storm expands over Pavel's face.

PAVEL
That kind of faggy thinking goes
against everything humanity does.
Science—out the door. Industry—
out the door. And ditto for
everything else in between.

Jake is at the boiling point. He has been set up. There is no mistaking the fury.

JAKE
Who are you callin a fag?

Pavel Kudlak

Out of respect for Jake, Pavel turns down his tone several decibels.

               PAVEL
I ain't calling you a fag. I'm just
relating how fucked up things can
be with that kind of horseshit in
our heads.

The sedan races around a corner. They're still cruising Chinatown.

               JAKE
That is not what I heard... okay,
okay. Let's just drop the whole
thing, all right.

They've dropped the whole thing. After a long moment... the Jag slows down noticeably, it is moving at a snail's crawl along the parked cars.

               PAVEL
Do you remember the situation I
spoke to you about earlier?

This gives Jake pause.

               JAKE
Sanchez?

Pavel Kudlak

Pavel makes no reply—eyes ahead.

Then, the Jaguar stops next to a bright red fire hydrant. About a hundred yards in the distance a worn-out sign reads, "WONG'S CHINESE GROCERIES."

                PAVEL
   There is my problem. The mutha'
   fucker is doing his shopping.

SANCHEZ, a middle-aged Oriental pegged with a Hispanic name, carefully picks through the cabbages on the vegetable stand situated in front of Wong's—your typical grocer with a base on the sidewalk, courtesy of city hall.

Pavel barely containing himself.

                PAVEL
             (continuing)
   Sanchez loves that bok choy. Must
   eat his vegetables every day or
   he'll never live to be one hundred.

Jake wakes from his stupor, becoming more excited. He peers at Sanchez.

JAKE
The little person in the canary
jacket, playing with the cabbages?
He was the driver of the white
van—hard to believe.

Both men stare straight ahead. Sanchez hasn't noticed them.

PAVEL
That is the rumor. Jake, you have
to promise me you'll be cool with
this dude. He is one bad
Vietnamese mutha' fucker and he's
always pissed about something.

JAKE
Hey, I'm cool. I'm a motherfuckin
ice cube. I ain't stupid I've heard
the stories.

The Jag is idling in drive; Pavel's foot is on the brake pedal. It hasn't moved an inch all this time.

JAKE
(continuing)
Well, park this vehicle and let's
chitchat with the infamous Mister
Sanchez.

Pavel Kudlak

PAVEL
Okay… yeah, in a second.
(then)
There won't be no chitchatting.

SUDDENLY… Pavel's right foot slams down on the gas pedal. The tires SPIN… as the Jaguar bolts toward Wong's—responding like a fine-tuned athlete.

A state of pure terror on Jake's face as he fumbles to pull his seat belt.

Pavel is completely unhinged.

PAVEL
(continuing, screams)
Sanchez, I hope you're wearing clean undies! It's judgement day!

EXT. "WONG'S" MARKET – NIGHT

The sedan mounts the curb in front of Wong's—aiming straight for Sanchez.

C.U. – SANCHEZ'S HAND
Drops a cabbage… pulls out a .38 Special from a shoulder holster… aims and FIRES three shots at the charging car. BANG! BANG! POW!

The Jag SMASHES into Sanchez, lifting him onto the hood. For a brief ugly moment, his contorted face peers into the vehicle—and we look into Pavel's crazed eyes.

Then... Sanchez vaults through the air like a soaring eagle run amuck... THROUGH the store's plate glass window and into the store itself... DEMOLISHING everything in sight.

INT. "WONG'S" MARKET – NIGHT

CHAOS reigns... customers SCREAM. Chinese ladies dive for cover as chunks of glass, mortar, cans, and vegetables become unidentified flying objects.

Sanchez is stretched out on the floor of the market among the many ruined crates and oranges. We see his face, he looks as dead as a doorplate.

The Jaguar sits motionless inside the store, briefly. Then... Pavel's hand cranks the gearbox into reverse and he proceeds to BURN more tire rubber than at Indianapolis on race day. The vehicle WHIPS out of Wong's and BARRELS down the curb and onto the street.

Pavel Kudlak

INT. "JAGUAR" – NIGHT – MOVING

The sedan is moving nicely along with the other vehicles of Chinatown—as if nothing has happened. Pavel has both hands firmly on the wheel, eyes straight ahead and minding his business. He's calm and collect. Jake, on the other hand, looks as if he's been through a full week of electroshock therapy.

> JAKE
> Are you outta your bleeding fuckin mind? I wanna get out of this carriage now… I said now.

Pavel throws a quick glance at Jake.

> PAVEL
> Right now? This minute? I can stop the car—I don't have a problem with that.

They are still inside Chinatown and not more than a block or two from Wong's.

> JAKE
> I cannot believe what just transpired. You killed a man based on a rumor—you sick motherfucker!

Pavel Kudlak

A state of apathy has set over Pavel. He turns a knob to start the windshield washer. The windshield clears of dirt, blood and debris. Jake looks at the windshield and... at Pavel, going back and forth.

PAVEL
(with a sigh)
Try to relax—take deep breaths.

From a distance, two police cruisers with their sirens ROARING whiz by. Followed by two ambulances.

JAKE
Fuck the deep breaths and fuck you. That poor bastard... no matter what he did—he did not deserve to die like that.

PAVEL
Oh, I see. Now you feel sorry for him.

JAKE
I ain't feelin sorry for nobody. But you do see that the matter ain't exactly honky dory.

The Jaguar exits Chinatown, finally.

Pavel Kudlak

> PAVEL
> The situation is not that bad, really.

Jake doesn't take the hint, he mutters on.

> JAKE
> Answer this: do you realize that a man was killed?

Almost instantly, Pavel SLAMS his palm into the steering wheel.

> PAVEL
> That's it… I'm done with ya, I'm done! We're dropping you off…

Pavel takes a moment to study Jake's condition and in the moment of a wink of an eye realizes that Jake is shot.

> PAVEL
> (continuing)
> You're bleeding! Why didn't you tell me?

Jake's nice suit is red with blood. Up until now, due to all the excitement and the effects of grandmother's brew, he wasn't aware of being shot.

> JAKE
> (realizing)
> Well, well, what d'ya know.
> Sanchez shot the wrong guy.

> PAVEL
> Give me your cell phone.

Jake takes out a cellular phone from an inside pocket and hands it to him.

Pavel starts punching numbers.

> PAVEL
> (continuing)
> The next time we happen to be in Chinatown, it will be my turn to take a bullet.

Jake throws him a look.

> PAVEL
> (continuing, into phone)
> Lara, sweetheart. I'm in a jar of pickles here with my good buddy, Jake. Listen to me carefully.
> (beat)
> I've got no time for small talk now.
> (MORE)

PAVEL (CONT'D)
Here is the situation—there's a patient on his way.
(beat)
No, it ain't me. Get some bandages and wraps ready and whatever else you can find to patch up a bullet wound. Antiseptics, painkillers… Honey, I can't go to a hospital with a thing like this. Try to understand the magnitude of this situation.
(then)
Okay, okay, I'm sorry for all the bad things I ever said to you. Don't cry. All right, can't explain further now. Put the garage door up. Kisses.

Pavel tosses down the cell phone.

JAKE
Are we cool?

PAVEL
You'll be fine. She's upset but reliable, like a Japanese watch. At one time, she worked in a vet's office—

Pavel Kudlak

> JAKE
> (interrupts)
> Wasn't she the receptionist?

> PAVEL
> Never mind that, she learned a whole bunch of stuff. Dogs, cats, people—it's all the same.

Pavel drives with both hands on the steering wheel obeying all traffic laws. He glances over at Jake—grimacing in pain. Clearly, the dope in Jake's system has worn off.

> JAKE
> Well, I'm grateful for that. But would you mind driving a little faster?

> PAVEL
> Sorry pal cannot do. We can't risk getting pulled over. Sit back, stretch out your legs, and enjoy the ride. Lara will patch you up and you'll be good as new. She's a genius with scissors, bandages, and tape.

Jake is more fidgety and nervous than usual. THEN... holding his shoulder, he lurches his head to the rear of the car... AND sees a Crown Victoria with a shiny ornament on its rooftop sitting directly behind them.

Suddenly, panic is written all over Jake's face. He quickly turns to face the front, breathing rapidly.

                JAKE
        Hey, Mister-Know-It-All, there's a
        cop on our tail.

Pavel glances nervously at the rearview mirror. A lone officer sits inside the Crown Vic.

                PAVEL
        Hang loose, baby. That man don't
        know squawk about us. He's
        probably looking for a place to take
        a leak.

A moment later, we hear the siren BLARING.

Jake swiftly spins around.

                JAKE
        Goddammit!

Pavel double-checks his mirror. The rooftop bubble is lit up like a Christmas tree.

Pavel Kudlak

Pavel casually pulls the strap of his seat belt snug and STOMPS on the accelerator. The Jaguar easily SPEEDS away from the police car, burning up pavement. He's driving like a mad Italian: racing up and down grades and dodging cars and trucks.

The Crown Vic gives chase.

The speedometer needle of the Jaguar rests on "100." Pavel barely negotiating a hairpin turn... the tires SQUEAL piercingly. Then... an oncoming Chevy convertible does the Jag SLIP SIDE... causing the Chevy to lose control and CRASH into a fire-plug. The fire hydrant BURSTS... flooding the intersection and the top down Chevy. The driver and passenger of the Chevy are soaked.

After a beat... the Jaguar runs a red light and almost mows down a jogger, crossing on a green. The jogger dives into the bushes, barely avoiding becoming hamburger meat.

The police cruiser follows and SKIDS SIDEWAYS into the intersection... becoming a near side RAMMING POST for a pick-up truck. Finally... the cruiser comes to rest, out of action. Black smoke billows from its hood.

Pavel Kudlak

The lone officer exits the disabled vehicle, pulls out his service revolver and FIRES several shots at the speeding Jag.

HOOTS of laughter and cheering erupts from both men.

At last... the Jag pulls into a quiet residential neighborhood. THEN... a garage door comes down behind the vehicle.

INT. OFFICE (DOJO) – DAY

SENSEI DAN, a 47-year-old karate master with a shaven head and tattoos, wearing a Tigers baseball cap, sits at a table doing paperwork.

A softball and a red and white paneled belt rest on his desk—a testament to his love of karate and softball. Numerous trophies are perched high on a shelf. The window blinds and the door of the office are wide open.

In the background, we hear POUNDING on a heavy bag.

Sensei Dan stares out through the big plate windows of the office unto the floor of his dojo.

Pavel Kudlak

INT. TRAINING HALL (DOJO) – DAY

The actual training area of the dojo is large, spotless and airy. Framed photographs of venerated karate masters line the front wall of the training hall. Various photographs of the club's fighters line another wall. Near the back of the room hang numerous heavy bags of various sizes and shapes.

We see about a half-dozen students dressed in traditional white karate uniforms training on their own.

Pavel, wearing a black belt around his waist, is training alone, putting together some impressive KICKS on a heavy banana bag.

Then... a brown belt approaches Pavel, bows and whispers something to him. We don't hear what the student says.

INT. OFFICE (DOJO) – DAY (LATER)

Sensei Dan and Pavel sit casually in the office sipping hot coffee and eating bagels. Pavel is still in his karate uniform. Sensei Dan's baseball cap sits on the table. The door of the office is closed. The mood is relaxed.

Pavel Kudlak

Occasionally, Sensei Dan looks out a window onto the floor of the training hall. Apparently, he has a lot on his mind.

> SENSEI DAN
> I'm not going to browbeat you, Pavel. That is not my style. As you know, karate has its roots in China. And in ancient China, the master of the dojo was responsible for the conduct of his students. I take this responsibility seriously. If a student brought shame unto himself, this reflected on the master. Normally, you would be required to resign from the dojo. No exceptions were made.

Pavel is all ears; he doesn't move a muscle.

> SENSEI DAN
> (continuing)
> However, this ain't ancient China and I'm not Chinese. Nor do I believe we should be slaves to tradition. A martial artist must be flexible in mind, body, and spirit. This is what my teachers taught me.

PAVEL
Yes, sir.

SENSEI DAN
I suggest you contact his family. Respect their wishes and honor them. You're doing this for them and for yourself. I expect you to excel in your training. I'm a follower of traditional ideals. My job is to change people. Soon, my candle will burn out... you will carry the flame.

Pavel stands and bows to his teacher.

SENSEI DAN
Now go.

Sensei Dan returns to the paperwork.

INT. BLACK SEDAN – NIGHT – MOVING

A luxury sedan with tainted windows travels along a busy street in the downtown corridor. An imposing Samoan bodyguard, known as TELICO, is doing double duty as the driver. Telico barely fits in the driver's seat. His suit looks to be at least two sizes too small for his frame.

The car's stereo is PLAYING Island Music in the background.

Jaws reclines comfortably in the back of the sedan. He shows off a cheap three-piece suit with all kinds of accessories around his wrists and neck. He has some sort of listening device stuck in one ear and a miniature microphone placed near his lips.

>   JAWS
> Please turn the thing off it's
> unsettling my nerves.

Jaws stares out the window of the sedan. We no longer hear Island Music in the background.

EXT. LITTLE ITALY – NIGHT

A typical street in the Italian section of the city. Specialty stores, boutiques, and restaurants line the path. It's a beehive of activity.

Then...

An off-road 4x4 pick-up carrying tons of caked mud on its fenders and tires THUNDERS by the luxury sedan.

INT. BLACK SEDAN – NIGHT – MOVING

Jaws comes alive… makes note of the muddy 4x4 motoring by.

                JAWS
           (into the mic)
    I'll take over now. Subject vehicle
    in view. Cut the cord on my
    mark… stand by.
           (to Telico)
    Follow the mud.

The sedan moves along with traffic. The truck is not more than half a block in front of us… Telico closing the distance without realizing.

                JAWS
           (continuing)
    Don't get too close. Fall back.

We drop back.

EXT. LITTLE ITALY – NIGHT

The 4x4 makes a right hand turn unto a tree-lined boulevard and slows down.

After a moment, the black sedan makes the same right turn and slows down. Then the sedan finds a vacant parking spot and pulls in sharply.

After a beat... the 4x4 pulls into an empty spot in front of a restaurant.

Then... Spunky and BIKER JOE, his passenger, excitedly exit the off-road vehicle. Biker Joe, like Spunky, is also a former biker and he's just as big as Spunky but he prefers to be clean-shaven. Each is showing off designer blue jeans accentuated by black leather vest and cowboy boots. Clearly, these fellows are no fashion aficionados.

They strut into the restaurant.

INT. "MARIO'S STEAK HOUSE" – NIGHT

A quiet, traditional Italian eatery with red and white checkered tablecloths and white cotton napkins. Several large photographs of Italy line the walls.

Spunky and Biker Joe sit at a table near the rear of the steak house, facing the bar. They are watching the football game on television.

The WAITER arrives to drop off their menus. He lingers for a long moment making small talk—we don't hear them.

EXT. / INT. "MARIO'S STEAK HOUSE" – NIGHT – TRACKING

A white cargo van SCREECHES to a stop in front of the restaurant.

ASSASSIN #1 and ASSASSIN #2 quickly exit the vehicle. Both Assassins are wearing identical overcoats, fedora, and sunglasses. It's hard to tell them apart.

We MOVE WITH them into the restaurant.

ALMOST IMMEDIATELY, the Assassins open their overcoats and each pulls out an identical sawed-off shotgun.

                ASSASSIN #1
        (screams)
    Nobody move. This is a goddamn
    robbery. Do as I say or I'll blow
    your head off.
        (points to a table)
    You and the misses, get under that
    fuckin table. Now… move.

The terrified couple crouch under the dining table as ordered. The other diners are too petrified to move or speak.

Both Assassins march toward Spunky and Biker Joe.

> ASSASSIN #2
> (loudly, to Spunky)
> Don't even think about it, cowboy.
> I wanna see your motherfuckin
> hands. Now stand up slow with
> your hands in the air.

Spunky and Biker Joe slowly leave their seats, with their hands in the air. The Waiter's hands are already up—he doesn't need to be told.

> SPUNKY
> I have real cash in the truck. I'm
> going to put my hands in my
> pocket to get out keys.

> ASSASSIN #2
> (screams)
> Do not move a fuckin nose hair.

Spunky's hands stay put.

> BIKER JOE
> (anxiously)
> I have a little girl... let's talk this
> over.

Both Assassins casually assume a menacing position in front of the trio. Their legs are wide apart shotguns pointing.

We see perspiration on the face of Assassin #2. Everybody is tense... a moment of hesitation... THEN... all hell BREAKS loose.

C.U. – THE ASSASSINS BLAST AWAY
As if at a carnival shooting gallery.
BANG! BANG! BANG! KABOOM! POW!

After a long moment.

It's a massacre—blood and guts everywhere. Spunky, Biker Joe and the unlucky Waiter are dead on the floor, riddled with bullet holes.

Patrons are cowering under tables, CRYING and SCREAMING.

> ASSASSIN #1
> (screams)
> Shut the fuck up.

Some diners actually obey him and stop crying and screaming.

Both Assassins quickly tuck their weapons under their overcoats... and we MOVE WITH them as they exit the restaurant and hop into the waiting cargo van.

INT. BLACK SEDAN – NIGHT – MOVING (LATER)

Several blocks away, the luxury sedan sits idling in the parking lot of a church. Jaws is listening to the news of the execution.

> JAWS
> (into the mic)
> I copy that, Roger. Good job. Out.
> (to Telico)
> I'll give you a chance to win back your five hundred—let's go out to the late-night driving range.

Telico glances up into the rearview mirror. We see Jaws gazing out the window of the sedan, looking at nothing in particular. Telico pushes a black button on the steering wheel. We HEAR Island Music in the background as the vehicle forces its way into heavy traffic.

Pavel Kudlak

INT. GRANDSTAND – NIGHT

We're at a racetrack jam packed with spectators. A water truck is spraying the surface. Several standardbreds are tied to jog carts while others are poised in front of race bikes—doing their last warm up prior to racing.

Pavel and Jake stand at a small table facing the oval munching on cheeseburgers and French fries and guzzling cold beer. Both men are dressed in sport jackets and slacks, with the shirt buttoned all the way to the top.

Pavel picks up the program and leafs through it as he sips his drink.

> PAVEL
> Pretty N Fast will wire this bunch;
> I feel it in my bones.

> JAKE
> (a puzzled look)
> I thought it was a fixed—

> PAVEL
> (interrupts)
> Never mind that. Why do you
> have to ruin a good Zen moment?
> Look at her last line.

Slides it across... Jake's nose is now in the program—he's studying the past performance lines of racehorses.

> PAVEL
> (continuing)
> You're lookin' at the wrong one...
> look at the number two. She
> parked much of the race last time
> and still managed to finish fourth
> by two lengths.

Jake checks out her last line using his right index finger as a guide—experiencing the Zen moment.

> JAKE
> The driver change can't hurt.

Jake looks up at the infield tote board. We see that the bets are scattered all over the place. The race favorite is the number three at odds of 7 to 2. Pretty N Fast, in the second slot, is going off at 8 to 1.

> JAKE
> (continuing)
> Why aren't they betting her?

Pavel throws a glance at the tote board.

Pavel Kudlak

PAVEL
Baby, who cares? This is Miss
Opportunity banging on our door.

Jake pulls out a fountain pen from his pocket, ready to write down numbers.

JAKE
How 'bout we box her with several
contenders.
(pause)
Give me some numbers to jot
down.

Pavel tears a big bite from his cheeseburger. Jake waits for him, conspicuously holding his pen.

PAVEL
How 'bout we get greedy! Key the
two with the six.

Jake scribbles the numerals we just heard into the program and draws a big circle around them.

JAKE
That all?

PAVEL
Are you gonna match my bet?

Pavel digs into his pocket and pulls out a large wad of cash.

Jake does a slow burn toward Pavel. He's nervous about betting a large sum of money on only two contenders in the race.

> PAVEL
> (continuing)
> I can't see anything else.

Jake grabs the bundle of green, pockets all and rushes off, clutching the program.

EXT. GRANDSTAND – NIGHT

Pavel is standing on the second floor, near the clubhouse turn. He's watching the trotters getting ready to race.

Jake waltzes to his side.

> JAKE
> We have a four hundred dollar ticket going: two and six straight. What's it paying?

Pretty N Fast trots in front of the grandstand.

Pavel Kudlak

PAVEL
That's her scoring. If she didn't
have a tail, I'd consider marriage.
>(then)

Our big ticket nets us twenty
grand. The reverse nets us over
seven G's.

JAKE
>(suddenly)

We don't have any fuckin reverse!

Pavel looks over at Jake for a long moment. The volcano is about to erupt.

PAVEL
I was very specific with you. I
said; hammer the two/six
combination. That means play the
reverse also.

The horses are approaching the starting gate.

JAKE
If that's what you wanted, why
didn't you say so?

Pavel is crumpling up the racing program.

JAKE
(continuing)
Fuck you, Kudlak. I would have gone back and changed it, if you had asked nice like. Now I ain't gonna.

Pavel is stunned; he cannot believe what he hears.

PAVEL
Fine! If you're prepared to lose your money, then I'm prepared to lose mine.

The trotters are lined up behind the wings… the starting gate begins to move forward, picking up speed.

ANNOUNCER (V.O.)
(over the p.a.)
The gate is rolling. It's fifth race post time—nine starters on the gate. And… there they go… they're off and trotting.

Pretty N Fast instantly shoots to the front of the pack.

Pavel Kudlak

PAVEL (O.S.)
Drive on, baby. Take no prisoners.

Suddenly, a trotter going to the top goes off stride. The driver tries to put him back on the trot without success. They fall back.

Now, we are in the thick of the action, getting a harness driver's view of the race. BRIGHT LIGHTS... CHIRPING... HEAVY BREATHING... WHEELS SPINNING. A horse is on the outside... another follows her cover.

ANNOUNCER (V.O.)
(over the p.a.)
Heading to the three-quarter pole...
Pretty N Fast is on top by two...
Canbe Glory is rushing on the outside...

JAKE (O.S.)
We got easy fractions.

At the top of the lane, they are four horses across.

PAVEL (O.S.)
We're gonna lose the race!

ANNOUNCER (V.O.)
(over the p.a.)
And… at the wire… it's Pretty N Fast—a gate to wire performance.

It's a photo for place between saddlecloth numbers six and three. Then... the official sign lights up with the results: "2-6-3."

Both gamblers jump up and down with excitement, grinning as if they won the mega-million lottery.

Several of the revelers tear up their tickets and toss 'em on the ground.

JAKE
We are kings!

PAVEL
She's a machine. C'mon, admit it.

JAKE
Okay, you're a bloody genius.
(under his breath)
They sure make it look good.

INT. ESCALATOR (RACETRACK) – NIGHT

Pavel and Jake are riding up an escalator, smiling from ear to ear as they count their sizable haul.

                PAVEL
    I gotta see this motherfucker
    Angelo Fedele about the Sanchez
    situation. Ever hear of him, Jake?

                JAKE
        (suddenly annoyed)
    Hey, do not be bringin' up that
    matter with me, or we're going to
    be tangling in the octagon. I
    haven't slept a wink since and all
    'cause of your careless ass.

They finish stuffing their pockets with cash.

                PAVEL
    How many times do I have to
    apologize? I said I was sorry.

                JAKE
    All right, then. No, to answer your
    question. Who is he?

PAVEL
For your information, Angelo Fedele runs this stinking town. They call him "Jaws" on account of 'im being bit by a great white while scuba diving off the coast of Florida. The dude now walks with a limp 'cause of a chunk missing from his thigh. He has become fascinated with sharks ever since.

JAKE
How come you know so much about him?

Pavel doesn't answer.

JAKE
(continuing)
So what do we call him, "Jaws"?

The two men walk off the escalator and enter the clubhouse corridor.

INT. CORRIDOR (RACETRACK) – NIGHT

Pavel and Jake stride toward the clubhouse entrance. We track alongside.

> PAVEL
> I wouldn't recommend you call 'im Jaws unless you wanna be thrown into the bay with a freshly killed tuna tied to your waist. I heard he's done that to guys, just for sport.

Pavel throws a glance at Jake.

> PAVEL
> (continuing)
> All right then, you just hang low and let me do the talkin'. I've got it on good account that Jaws can help our situation.

> JAKE
> This rendezvous better not be a repeat of Chinatown, 'cause I'll bail out early if it's comin' to that.

Pavel rolls his eyes. It's another annoyance.

                    PAVEL
          Man, I'm offended. I ain't gonna
          mess up our relationship and all.

                    JAKE
          You're on notice and that's all I'm
          going to say on the subject.

                    PAVEL
          Hey, I wouldn't dream of fuckin
          you twice.
               (beat)
          All right, get serious now. Put
          your girly face on.

They enter the clubhouse.

INT. CLUBHOUSE (RACETRACK) – NIGHT

The room is tranquil and dignified. Antique chandeliers and furniture in the serenity of French blue and cream soothe the gamblers. Freshly cut long stemmed yellow tulips rest in crystal vases. The mutual tellers are plying their trade dressed in red vests and black bow tie.

Pavel and Jake stroll over to the maitre d'. Pavel leans forward and whispers something into his ear. The maitre d' escorts the two gamblers to a table near the finish line and splits.

Pavel and Jake now stand at attention near the table of Angelo Fedele, who has his back turned to us.

PAVEL
Mister Fedele.

Jaws looks up from his rack of lamb—he's still chewing food. Jaws wears a gold bracelet on one wrist, a Rolex on the other, and on a chain around his neck a triangular-shaped tooth of a great white.

JAWS
(smiles)
Boys, boys, boys. I've been expecting you. Well now, let me guess.
(to Pavel)
You are Marie-Karoline's grandson. The woman could not stop blabbering about you.
(to Jake)
And you must be his loyal partner in crime—

> PAVEL
> (interrupts)
> True on both counts, sir.

> JAWS
> Well, sit down fellas.

The two men take their seats as ordered.

> JAWS
> (continuing)
> This beautiful person is Jackie.

JACKIE smiles broadly. A sensual exotic brunette with full dark ruby lips—impeccably dressed in a black strapless evening gown with matching pearls. She picks at a veggie platter.

> PAVEL AND JAKE (O.S.)
> (in unison)
> Hi Jackie!

> JACKIE
> (amused)
> Hi fellas!

Jaws pours red wine for everybody except Jackie. She's sipping a chocolate milkshake.

EDDIE GREEN, the mayor, immediately gulps down his drink and places his empty glass on the table.

>   JAWS
> Have some more, Eddie.

Jaws fills Eddie's glass. The mayor looks like the greedy sort. He sports a plaid two-piece suit with an expensive tie that doesn't match. It's perfect for him.

Pavel checks out Jackie as she sips her milkshake. She looks up, ever so briefly.

Jaws hasn't noticed him staring at his date.

>   JAWS
>   (continuing, points)
>   That's Telico.

Telico, whom we met previously, acknowledges them with a grunt. He has a habit of standing erect no matter what he does—probably because of the tight suits he wears. Telico is never more than several feet from his master and he rarely smiles. But he's always polite.

JAWS
(continuing)
I'd be lost without him. Best darn driver I've had. An expert on everything from Mongolian beer to lead-free blinds. To top it all he makes one hell of lasagna.

PAVEL
You don't say, sir. I would never have guessed.

JAKE
Nor I and I'm a good cook. I love to make Italian dishes. I can usually pick out a good cook in a crowd, but I missed the big guy.

Jaws looks at Jake in disbelief.

JAKE
(continuing)
I would love to have his recipe for lasagna.

JAWS
(between bites)
I'm sure Telico wouldn't mind sharing.

Pavel Kudlak

A waiter brings a bottle of Tokaji Aszu, a topaz-colored dessert wine from Hungary.

Small port glasses are set for all. A waiter removes Jackie's milkshake glass. Then... plates of perfectly ripe peeled peaches arrive for all guests.

Jaws pours dessert wine into the mayor's glass. The mayor quickly makes short work of it and follows with a piece of peach.

Jaws looks up at Pavel.

>PAVEL
>Sir, the reason we're here—

>JAWS
>(interrupts)
>Pavel, did your late grandmother tell you 'bout the time she hitchhiked across the Middle East with only a sleeping bag?

>PAVEL
>No, it probably slipped her mind, sir.

                    JAWS
                (suddenly)
            Okay, cut the sir 'ing. I ain't no
            high school principal. Call me
            Angelo or better yet, Jaws.

Pavel and Jake exchange glances.

Jaws nods to Telico… he immediately appears at his side. Jaws hands him several tickets. Telico tucks them into his pocket… and splits.

                    JAWS
                (continuing)
            Don't you think I know why you're
            here? However, let's not talk shop
            during dinner it upsets my
            digestion.

He reaches for more peaches.

                    JACKIE
            Angelo, why don't you tell them
            something about sharks. I'm sure
            they'd love to hear about them.

Instantly, Jaws brightens up. Jackie knows precisely which buttons to push.

>   JAWS
> A splendid idea! Kids, you
> probably think I'm an eccentric
> fool, but we can learn so much
> from sharks. And they're not
> nearly as stupid as people.
>
>   JAKE
> Care to elaborate, sir.

Jaws gestures with a fork in his hand, indicating, "come closer." The men comply as ordered. Now they're closer to Jaws than they ever wanted to be.

>   JAWS
>   (whispers)
> We are not here to talk about
> sharks. We're here because you
> stepped in fresh cow dung.
>
>   JACKIE
> Angelo, you promised.

Jaws puts the fork down and leans back into his chair.

           JAWS
Jackie, these bums need to learn
the facts of life. They haven't
figured out that if you're going to
commit a crime in America, at
least pick one that's socially
acceptable. Then you can go on
TV and become a celebrity—a role
model.

          JACKIE
Is there nothing you can do?

The two men take that as their cue to lean back a little also.

           JAWS
        (to Pavel)
Motherfucker, killin Sanchez
doesn't get you on Oprah.

          JACKIE
Angelo!

           JAWS
        (to Jackie)
This is a bloody powder keg… it
needs care and nurturing.
          (MORE)

JAWS (CONT'D)
(then)
However, great delicacy has never been my forte.

Telico comes to the table and drops a stuffed envelope in front of Jaws. Then he moves away but stands nearby.

Jaws pushes the envelope in front of the mayor. The mayor does a quick glance around the room.

JAWS
(continuing, to Eddie)
Let the chief know I'm doing this my way. Will you do that for me, Eddie?

EDDIE
Of course, Angelo.

Eddie stuffs the envelope into his inside pocket and splits.

JAWS
(to Pavel)
I want you to understand something—things are always more complex than they appear.

Pavel Kudlak

We can see Pavel's eyelid fluttering nervously. A sad loneliness engulfs his face.

                    JAKE
    Mister Fedele, we'll be angels...
    choirboys.

A long beat... SUDDENLY, the maniacal side of Jaws erupts. He POUNDS the table hard with his fist, almost knocking it over. Tulips CRASH unto the floor, glasses and drinks TOPPLE over and plates FLY through the air.

The clubhouse is stunned silent. Everyone stops doing whatever... some guests stare in their direction.

Telico takes a position beside Jaws and casually unbuttons his suit jacket. We see a big, black .357 Magnum sitting in a shoulder holster.

                    JAWS
        (to a clubhouse patron)
    Mind your own business, asshole.

At once, the diner turns his head away.

                    PAVEL
        (blinking)
  Sir—

Pavel Kudlak

Jaws peers over at Pavel. Then he takes the wine bottle and slowly fills Pavel's glass.

> JAWS
> When I was young like you boys, I was full of dash and pizzazz. I thought I was going to make an impression, change the world… contribute to the arts and sciences—

Jaws pauses and stares out at the oval for a moment. He is lost in his own thought. An overwhelming distant look of regret comes over his face. His eyes are misty.

> PAVEL
> What happened?

Jaws stares across at Pavel.

> JAWS
> Then… nothing—zilch. Ideas need a push and a pull and mine lacked both. So now, now that I'm older and much fatter, I'm more afraid of boredom than of dying.

> JAKE
> I understand perfectly.

                    JAWS
Be quiet! Fellas, Darwin never
said, "Only the paranoid survive."
That was a fuckin businessman. In
America, we love achievement. If
you make a choice to be
something, even if it's to kill and
you stay true to those convictions,
you'll be honored and respected.

Jaws takes a deep breath and leans back into his chair. He waits for the two men to digest this new piece of information.

The men are studying him.

                    JAWS
                 (continuing)
I'll make it simple. I didn't wanna
bring up sharks again, but I guess I
need to. Do you know that the
unborn tiger shark pup, while in
the uterus, consumes his siblings as
these hatch one by one, until only
one survives ready to be born.
Now, that is what I call ensuring
your own survival.

Pavel and Jake exchange glances.

Pavel Kudlak

PAVEL
So the tiger shark is a cannibal—
before he is born.

Jaws takes a teaspoon off the table and CLANGS his water glass.

JAWS
That's my way of saying stay out
of Chinatown. I think you're smart
enough to figure out the rest.

JAKE
We've figured it out. Never again,
sir. I didn't care for Chinese food
anyway.

JAWS
You're beginning to annoy me.
   (then)
If there are no further questions, I
must bid you adieu.

Pavel and Jake rise to... exit.

Pavel Kudlak

EXT. NARROW STREET – DAY

A laid-back ethnic neighborhood. Wildly colored wooden frame homes, specialty shops, and all manner of pedestrians line the street.

Pavel exits a secondhand bookstore. He strolls along the sun-drenched street, humming softly to himself. We track alongside.

THEN... he notices Jackie striding along ahead of him... stunning in a navy blue leather slit dress, with matching leather gloves and a black beret teasingly angled to one side.

Pavel's strides shorten in length... he spies her from a short distance behind. She hasn't noticed him. Jackie moves energetically along... stopping occasionally to gaze into storefront windows and boutiques.

Before long... Jackie peers into the window of an upscale delicatessen... she enters. We gaze inside. The fat, jolly fellow working behind the counter is thrilled to see her. He smiles and gestures theatrically with his hands as he speaks with Jackie. She laughs along with the excited fella. We have no idea what they're talking about. Then, using a large butcher knife, we watch him cut a hunk of blue cheese.

Pavel Kudlak

Pavel stands in a doorway across the street, an air of overconfidence... studying Jackie's graceful movements as she makes her purchase.

INT. "THE CHEESELADY" DELI – DAY

A typical Italian delicatessen, crammed to the rafters with a variety of ready-made food. Various assortment of cheese hang enticingly from the ceiling.

C.U. – JACKIE
Suddenly senses that she is watched.

Pavel is leaning against a hydro pole smoking a cigarette... staring at Jackie. They lock eyes for a moment. Pavel remains aloof... then... Jackie blinks, smiles faintly. After a beat... she exits the deli.

EXT. NARROW STREET – DAY

Jackie glides along, lugging a small bag of groceries. Pavel tracks her from a short distance. Then, she glances over her shoulder and makes a turn into a pedestrian-only laneway. A moment later... Pavel makes the same turn. Soon, he's virtually on her heels.

Pavel Kudlak

EXT. JACKIE'S BUILDING – DAY

Jackie and Pavel arrive at the same time—if we didn't know any better, we'd think they were a couple.

Previously, her building was a publisher's warehouse—now it serves as an apartment building, the kind we are seeing more frequently, especially in the downtown corridor.

Jackie casually passes her grocery bag to Pavel and in a flash his defiance disappears. She reaches into her handbag for a key. They have yet to say a single word to each other. Both are content to let the situation speak for itself. They enter Jackie's building.

INT. FREIGHT ELEVATOR – DAY

Jackie presses button number "4" on the elevator panel. The elevator starts with a JERK, CLANGS and STOPS.

Pavel shifts his feet. Jackie smiles and punches button number "4" again. The elevator CLAMORS up the floors… as Pavel and Jackie gaze into each other's eyes.

Eventually the elevator stops. Jackie SLIDES the elevator door open. They exit.

INT. STUDIO/LIVING AREA (JACKIE'S LOFT) – DAY

Clearly, Jackie's apartment serves as both her studio and residence. Pavel looks around. It's tastefully decorated, but it is unmistakably an artist's studio. Various paints, brushes, tools, and rolls of canvas lay about. Numerous oils and watercolors decorate the walls. Art objects from Africa, Asia, and the Middle East are scattered throughout.

> PAVEL
> Have you lived here long?

> JACKIE (O.S.)
> Oh… about six months, maybe seven. Why do you ask?

> PAVEL
> Just curious. I don't know why…
> I suppose I'm trying to make small talk during an awkward moment.

Jackie stands in the living area of the loft.

JACKIE
Are you sure? I took this place
after my separation. One needs to
live somewhere.

She brushes aside her long hair. A moment of reflection. Pavel studying her.

PAVEL
You're single.

Jackie just looks at him. Pavel strolls over to a large kilim hung on a wall of the living area.

JACKIE
I bought that piece in Anatolia last
year… better to hang—than to
trample on.

He wanders through the living area and steps into the studio portion of the loft. We don't see Jackie.

Now, he studies an unfinished still life charcoal in progress.

JACKIE (O.S.)
(continuing)
We left each other more than a
dozen times.

Pavel Kudlak

Jackie is standing behind a makeshift curtain changing her clothes. We see her shapely outline clearly through the curtain fabric.

A long beat. Then... Jackie appears in hip huggers and a tight blouse... walks to the studio portion near Pavel.

>JACKIE
>(continuing)
>My husband and I became too accustomed to one another.
>(beat)
>We were probably too much in love—with everything and everybody.

Pavel removes a large pink bed sheet covering an unfinished sculpture of a male. He stares at the unfinished nude for a long moment.

>JACKIE
>(continuing)
>You won't find this conversation too interesting, Pavel—with your education and background.

Jackie grabs a chisel and hammer sitting nearby and commences CHISELING the nude male.

PAVEL
On the contrary—

She's hardly listening... CHIPS away.

JACKIE
(working)
Love can sometimes get in the way of things.
(then)
Every so often, I take him out into the light and bring him alive. Art is affirmation... I heard he's living in Brazil... with a Mexican Gypsy. Life can be funny.

PAVEL
(searching for words)
I've... I've never been to Brazil.

Jackie looks at him intently. Pavel flashing a blinding smile.

JACKIE
(working)
I suppose you find me attractive and somewhat vulnerable. And you probably think I'm an easy lay and I probably am.

PAVEL
Quite the opposite. Of course, I—

JACKIE
(interrupts)
You don't have to deny it, Pavel.

Jackie grabs the pink bed sheet and covers the nude male. Then she wanders away.

Pavel stares at the mass of pink covering the sculpture. After a beat... Jackie arrives with refreshments. She places Pavel's drink on a hand-painted trunk—of pines and riders on horseback.

PAVEL
May I ask you a question?

Jackie ambles to an easel... begins to work on a watercolor, of a sailboat caught in rough seas.

Pavel watching her work.

After a beat.

JACKIE
What did you want to ask?

Pavel Kudlak

Pavel saunters to her side—now facing the watercolor. He watches the maturation take place before his eyes as Jackie energetically brushes on the blues and greens.

>PAVEL
>Frankly, I've forgotten the question.

>JACKIE
>(working)
>Watercolor is interesting, don't you think? The water adds dimension.

>PAVEL
>(into it)
>It's the medium of the gods. Unfortunately, I'm only good with a ballpoint pen.

Jackie throws him a glance.

>PAVEL
>(continuing)
>Do you always agonize about the past? I mean, why you care that he's with a Mexican Gypsy.

She looks at him for a long moment; touched by his sentiment.

JACKIE
I trust you're referring to my estranged husband. It is not agony when one takes each day as it comes, one at a time, piece by piece.

She returns to the watercolor, brushing colors unto her seas.

PAVEL
I don't understand.

He now stands beside the easel, facing Jackie.

JACKIE
(working)
I remember seeing a documentary film about Mikhail Gorbachev coming to New York and there were two elderly women waiting for hours in the rain to see him. Some reporter asked them why they were there. And one said, "Well... he's trying, that's all anyone can do." I think that describes my life. I'm trying.
(beat)
Why don't you tell me something about the poet, Pavel Kudlak!

Pavel Kudlak

She puts her brushes down and waits.

> **PAVEL**
> (sighs)
> Actually, there is not much to tell. Since you insist… what would you like to know… whether I screw on a first date, masturbate all day… or attend protest marches?

> **JACKIE**
> Hmm… I'm not sure what I want to know. Start with whatever you like and work your way up. We have all night.

> **PAVEL**
> All right… I stopped believing in fairy tales, ghosts and humanity a long time ago… out of necessity. I didn't quit believing—just saw no reason to continue doing so.

He has Jackie's attention now.

> **JACKIE**
> Oh, this is serious tell me something about yourself jabber.

Pavel Kudlak

PAVEL
Suppose it is. It's that I no longer need to be deep. I just want to be very wide—like the Grand Canyon, so that it takes a long time to walk around me.

A momentary pause.

CLOSE ON JACKIE
As she slowly unfastens a button of her blouse.

PAVEL
(continuing)
I love your work, especially the watercolors. I mean, I appreciate art... much more than the average bloke. For me, since I'm a Czech, the line between art and life is thin.

Jackie glances at him... THEN... she loosens another catch of her blouse, seductively exposing the tops of her breasts.

JACKIE
So, my art intrigues you.

Pavel plays a soft hand against Jackie's cheek... then... he lays his hand to her breast... they ravish each other aggressively... lips locked together in harmony... his mouth covering her face and neck. We see the sailboat in rough seas shimmer.

C.U. – JACKIE
Urgently unbuttons his shirt... kneels in front of him... her long fingers peeling off his slacks... we see the back of Jackie's bare shoulders... Pavel's fingers gripping her long curls.

INT. DINING AREA (JACKIE'S LOFT) – DAY

Jackie and Pavel sit at a table. Pavel is lounging in a big chair scanning the newspaper, he's wearing a thick bathrobe. Jackie is dressed in a ratty T-shirt and gym pants. Pancakes, sausages, and eggs are on plates.

JACKIE
More coffee?

Pavel nods his head, indicating yes. She pours more coffee into his mug.

PAVEL
Dankeschon.

Then... Jackie holds up a large plate of pancakes and sausages.

JACKIE
Try some pancakes, my own
recipe... banana raisin.

Pavel tosses the paper down and dishes several pancakes and sausages unto his plate... then he drowns everything with Canadian maple syrup. He takes a mouthful.

PAVEL
Damn, this is good. I feel as if
you're deliberately fattening me
up.

JAKIE
That's been my plan all along.
(then)
Please tell me more.

Pavel pushes away the plate of food. A great sadness engulfs his face.

Pavel Kudlak

INT. STUDIO/LIVING AREA (JACKIE'S LOFT) – DAY

Now he stands in front of the rug, staring into its intricate pattern. Jackie is next to him.

> JACKIE
> I shouldn't have brought it up.

> PAVEL
> It's not your fault… What's that famous line of Nietzsche, "That which doesn't destroy us, makes us… stronger?"
> (then)
> Shrinks could not help…

He picks up a carved giraffe sitting on a table nearby and just looks at it. A moment later, he puts the object down—pulling his self together.

> PAVEL
> (continuing)
> A casualty of living careless—in a world of murderers, gangsters and pirates…
> (beat)
> At one time, I accepted it… now, I'm not so sure.

Pavel Kudlak

EXT. CITY PARK – DAY

We're in a large park situated only a mile or so from the highway—with a pond smack dab in the middle. Numerous duck and swan swim leisurely about. Joggers jog and lovers stroll, as children chase squirrels and make merry.

Pavel ambles to the edge of the pond... licking an ice cream cone, carrying a plastic shopping bag. He finishes the cone, opens the plastic bag and tosses breadcrumbs at the duck wading in the pool. The duck scurry to the pond's edge to snatch the morsels of stale bread... then, Pavel shakes the bag over the edge of the pond, emptying it out. The duck take whatever they can and swim elsewhere on the pond in search of more free food.

Pavel reclines on the grass to catch a much needed snooze... staring up at the blue sky.

SUDDENLY... GUNSHOTS pierce the silence.

Stunned, Pavel rolls several times on the grass to avoid being filled with lead. He looks up to see who's shooting. He thinks he knows where the shots are coming from. In the distance, we see a dude with a rifle taking aim—crouched behind the doors of a full size silver SUV, wearing an overcoat and fedora.

THEN, two more shots RING OUT. Terrified, Pavel bolts behind a large oak near the pond. We see slugs SLAM into its bark.

THEN... he makes a desperate last minute dash into the pond, SPLASH. A million bullets PUNCH the water as he swims underwater for what seems like an eternity. We see Pavel's exhausted face underwater, his eyes are wide open and he's about to burst from lack of oxygen.

FINALLY... he crawls out of the water on the other side of the pond... GASPING for air, soaking wet. He darts to safety behind the thick bushes. The gunshots cease.

INT. SILVER SUV – DAY – MOVING

Two guys in identical overcoats and fedora, traveling on a highway in a shiny rubber tire fortress. A rifle sits between them. Assassin #2 is doing the driving.

ASSASSIN #2
Did you get 'im?

ASSASSIN #1
I killed everything in that fuckin water. It'll take a hundred years for that pond to recover. Drive me home I'm tired.

Assassin #2 throws him a glance. Then he casually looks in the rearview mirror and does a double take. A green Jaguar is advancing on them like a cruise missile.

ASSASSIN #2
(screams)
The fuckin bastard... he's behind us.

Assassin #1 whips his body around and sees the bad news.

ASSASSIN #2
(continuing)
You never could hit anything.

BAM! Assassin #2 SLUGS his unsuspecting partner with a vicious back fist. Knocks him out cold. The head of Assassin #1 just lies there—no longer moving.

Next, he punches the gas pedal. The SUV is moving as fast as any overweight vehicle can go. Assassin #2 struggles to keep the shiny side up.

The Jaguar is closing fast.

INT. "JAGUAR" – DAY – MOVING

Now the Jag is motoring in the passing lane. In no time at all, it's alongside the SUV. The vehicles are cruising side-by-side, doors touching.

A big truck is heading straight for the Jag. The truck driver blasts his HORN. We see the ugly face of Assassin #2—he's grinning. Not giving an inch.

BUT before the assassin can do anything further, the passenger side window of the Jaguar comes down and Pavel FIRES two rapid shots into the SUV… Assassin #2 slumps dead over the steering wheel—blood seeping from his ear.

Instantly, Pavel slams his foot on the brake pedal and barely makes it behind the SUV as the 18-wheeler ROARS by.

Pavel Kudlak

EXT. HIGHWAY – DAY

A moment later, the out of control SUV runs off the road and CRASHES violently into a large tree. THEN... the vehicle EXPLODES—just like in the movies. The flames are about a hundred feet high, or so it seems. It is not a pretty sight.

INT. POLICE HEADQUARTERS – DAY

Pavel sits at a table in an interrogation room of the police department, his clothes are still wet. There is not much in the room except for a desk and a telephone hanging on a wall. The door is closed.

SERGEANT O'MALLEY, a softhearted member of the homicide division stands across the table from Pavel. O'Malley wears a short-sleeve shirt without a tie and jacket—he hates formality. His service revolver is holstered. He looks like he was always a cop.

The door opens and HENDERSON enters the room. Henderson is a skinny, fast-talking detective with curly red hair. He looks like a college geek rather than a seasoned cop. Although there's little about Henderson that says

Pavel Kudlak

he should be a cop—everyone in his family is a cop.

>HENDERSON
>Pavel, you've become a fixture here. I see you more than I see my wife.

>SERGEANT O'MALLEY
>Henderson, tell the mayor to charge him rent!

The two detectives snicker.

>HENDERSON
>This time you're in big trouble, Kudlak. What were you doing in Chinatown last Friday?

>PAVEL
>(mockingly)
>I think I was having Peking duck.

>SERGEANT O'MALLEY
>(starting toward Pavel)
>Listen son, your rights have been read to you and you agreed to answer our questions.
>(MORE)

                    SERGEANT O'MALLEY
                    (CONT'D)
          You know we're taping this
          interview and you declined to have
          your attorney present. So, answer
          our questions and in return, we will
          have the charges reduced to
          involuntary manslaughter. But
          don't be fuckin smart with me; this
          ain't television.

The telephone RINGS.

                    SERGEANT O'MALLEY
                        (continuing)
          Henderson, get that.

Henderson picks up the receiver.

                    HENDERSON
                        (into phone)
          This is Henderson... yes, captain...
          we just started the interview...
                        (looks at Pavel)
          He's not talking—
                        (then)
          Captain, there must be some
          mistake, captain—yes sir.

Henderson SLAMS down the phone.

Pavel Kudlak

SUDDENLY... he picks up the receiver again and begins BEATING it mercilessly against the wall unit. Finally, the wall unit and the receiver are in several pieces, dangling from the wall.

Henderson glares at Pavel.

>HENDERSON
>(continuing)
>Sergeant, we have to let Kudlak go. Captain's orders.

O'Malley just looks at Henderson.

Pavel looks up.

>HENDERSON
>(continuing)
>Did you hear me?

>SERGEANT O'MALLEY
>I heard plenty... Twenty fuckin years of busting my ass, doing stakeouts and eating bologna sandwiches and it comes down to this... Kudlak, you're not getting off that easy—

Pavel Kudlak

O'Malley FLINGS himself across the table at Pavel. Both men land on the floor and begin to do their version of the mixed martial arts craze.

The skinny cop rushes in to break up the fight... and, as Pavel is about to land a blow on O'Malley, Henderson draws his pistol and puts the gun to Pavel's temple.

>HENDERSON
>Move and you're dead, punk.

Pavel looks at the gun—he dare not move. Blood trickles from his nose.

>HENDERSON
>(continuing)
>That's better. Now sit in that
>fuckin chair and don't move.

Pavel sits as ordered.

>SERGEANT O'MALLEY
>(gets up, out of breath)
>What are we going to do with him?

>HENDERSON
>We've done all we can do in this
>case. You wanna throw away
>twenty years and a shitty pension.

Pavel Kudlak

> SERGEANT O'MALLEY
> Get the hell out of here, Kudlak,
> before I change my mind.

Pavel shifts in his chair—he doesn't move.

> PAVEL
> I'm not leaving until I get some
> answers.

> HENDERSON
> (angrily)
> What's he talking about?

> SERGEANT O'MALLEY
> (to Henderson)
> He thinks we sit here all day
> drinking coffee and eating cream
> cheese bagel.

> HENDERSON
> So!

> SERGEANT O'MALLEY
> Kudlak, listen up. Your wonderful
> father killed your mother during an
> argument. The district attorney
> will not go forward with it because
> the DNA from the semen does not
> match—

> HENDERSON
> (interrupts)
> Besides, Mister Kudlak is sitting
> right where the courts will send
> him anyway.

Pavel just glares at them.

A KNOCK on the door. An officer enters and speaks with O'Malley. We don't hear them. The officer splits.

O'Malley studies Pavel for a long moment.

> SERGEANT O'MALLEY
> Pavel, your father is dead. He
> hung himself at the hospital. I'm
> sorry, kid.

Pavel droops in his chair unable to move or speak—he looks utterly defeated.

> SERGEANT O'MALLEY
> (continuing)
> I said he's dead. I'm sorry.
> (pause)
> You should connect your
> telephone. Why is it disconnected
> anyway?

Pavel Kudlak

Pavel, trembling, slowly rises to his feet. He thrusts both hands at the air, mouth open. His eyes are moist.

> PAVEL
> (desperately)
> No! It's not fair... we weren't finished.

O'Malley studies him... after a beat... O'Malley walks to the door, opens it and sticks his head out.

> SERGEANT O'MALLEY
> Brown, get me the Kudlak file, on the double.

Henderson merely shakes his head.

After a beat... an officer enters the room and hands O'Malley a large file folder and splits. O'Malley throws the file on the table.

> SERGEANT O'MALLEY
> (continuing)
> Happy reading, kid.

The two detectives walk out.

Pavel stares at the file of reports, leads, and briefs. Then he dumps the entire contents of the file onto the table. He begins to read the mountain of reports—jumping from one document to the next. After a beat... he tears a page from a report, folds it neatly and puts it in his pants pocket.

THEN... he FURLS the mountain to the floor. Reports, briefs and other documents are scattered all over the room.

EXT. CEMETERY – DAY (RAINING)

Jake and Lara stand among other mourners near an open grave. It's about 10:00 in the morning with a slow drizzle coming down. Still there are a good number of folks in attendance.

An ELDERLY PRIEST stands under an umbrella clutching a Bible to his chest. Jackie stands alone nearby, occasionally dabbing her eyes with a tissue. Then... the attendants lower the casket into its final resting place.

>   LARA
>   (whispers to Jake)
>   Where is Pavel? I'm worried.

Pavel Kudlak

> ELDERLY PRIEST (O.S.)
> O Lord, we pray thee, loose thy
> servant from every bond, and
> receive his soul in peace, granting
> him rest in thine eternal dwelling
> with all thy saints, by the grace of
> thine only Son our Lord Jesus
> Christ.

Several mourners exchange curious glances with each other. After a beat... Jackie rushes off from the grave site, before the service concludes.

INT. LIVING ROOM (PAVEL'S APT.) – DAY

Pavel brings down a dusty cardboard box from the top shelf of the hall closet and sets it on the coffee table. He riffles through the contents of the box. Clearly, the container holds mostly old papers, letters, and notes. Pavel reads the papers quickly, tossing those that do not interest him onto the floor.

All of a sudden, a particular letter engrosses him... he reads it again. Although we do not see the actual text of this dispatch, we see Pavel's lower lip begin to quiver. He puts the note down... grabs an old address book from inside the cardboard box and frantically flips through its pages. Then he rips a page from the old directory and stuffs the piece of paper into his shirt pocket.

INT. BEDROOM (PAVEL'S APT.) – DAY

Pavel is in undergarments. He grabs a fresh white shirt from a hanger in the closet and puts it on. Then he pulls out a pristine two-piece business suit from the closet and places the jacket on the bed. The pants go on.

He opens the top drawer of the dresser and pulls out a shoulder holster holding a .45 caliber semi-automatic pistol. We see him putting on the shoulder holster. Then... he takes the address page from the pocket of the dirty shirt and stuffs it into his jacket pocket.

INT. LIVING ROOM (PAVEL'S APT.) – DAY

Pavel sits on the leather couch. His jacket drapes a chair nearby. A cigarette burns in an ashtray on the coffee table. Pavel opens a small packet of aluminum foil and pulls out a chunk of dark hashish. He breaks off a piece of hash and places it on the head of the burning cigarette. The hash begins to burn. Then... he takes several tokes from the burning hash. Soon... it's obvious that he has a good buzz going. Then, he puts out the cigarette... grabs his jacket and... dashes out of his apartment as if it were on fire, leaving everything as is.

INT. ATRIUM (CONDOMINIUM) – DAY

We're in the lobby of a typical upscale residential condo. Chrome, glass and leather everywhere.

Pavel punches the lobby buzzer: RING! RING! RING!

> MALE VOICE (V.O.)
> (over the intercom)
> Yes... who is it?

> PAVEL
> (into the intercom)
> I'm looking for Aleksandr Lazic. I must speak with you...

> MALE VOICE (V.O.)
> (over the intercom)
> There's no one here by that name. Leave me alone.

He holds his finger down on the buzzer: DING DONG!

> MALE VOICE (V.O.)
> (continuing, over the intercom)
> Go away! Leave me in peace.

> PAVEL
> (into the intercom)
> I'm afraid I can't do that.

Then... the front door is BUZZED open. Pavel enters the apartment building.

INT. HALLWAY (CONDOMINIUM) – DAY

The elevator doors open. Pavel steps off and walks down the carpeted corridor, lined with gothic glass fixtures. Looking at door numbers.

He stands in front of a door numbered "701"... a moment of reflection... he BANGS on the door.

The faint sound of SHUFFLING feet... then a FUMBLING with keys.

INT. FOYER (APT. 701) – DAY

We're inside Lazic's pad. Various signs of the zodiac decorate the arched doorway of his apartment—its meaning is unclear.

ALEKSANDR LAZIC, a middle-aged male with graying hair, JERKS the noisy latch and opens the door to reveal Pavel standing in the hallway.

> LAZIC
> Do not stand there, boy. Welcome, welcome to my home—enter freely.

Pavel takes a small step forward, some hesitation.

Lazic is without a doubt an eccentric individual. A purple-colored V-shaped satin collar hangs magisterially on his shoulders over the white jacket of his two-piece suit. A golden astrological medallion dangles from his neck over the satin collar.

> LAZIC
> (continuing)
> I seldom have guests… I can't remember when I did.

Pavel steps inside… trying not to stare at Lazic's medallion.

Pavel Kudlak

INT. LIVING ROOM (APT. 701) – DAY

Pavel looks around—he's both shocked and curious. Lazic's residence is more of an underground temple than a home. A large hole in the easterly wall admits the sun—to reveal ritual pottery vessels and sacred art objects. An altar in purple and silver sits conspicuously at another end of the room. Candles of various shapes and sizes light up the room.

A look of morbid astonishment engulfs Pavel's face. He walks toward a wall depicting a young man in the act of slaying a bull with a sword. The figures accompanying the bull slaying represent constellations. Pavel stares at the picture.

>   LAZIC (O.S.)
>   For your information, that is not
>   some mindless depiction of animal
>   cruelty. Its meaning holds the key
>   to Mithras.
>   (then)
>   Snap out of it, boy.

Pavel throws him a quick glance.

After a beat... Pavel examines a fantastic animal mask of a raven. Other animal masks of a wolf and serpent lay close-by. He's catching on.

PAVEL
You're a fuckin pagan… Mithras was a pre-Christian god.

LAZIC
Ah, very good… I'm impressed, but then I shouldn't be.

Lazic turns toward the altar… lighting several small candles.

LAZIC
(continuing)
We seek no miracles, only the signage… and have no bishops… hate can be an enormously satisfying emotion.

PAVEL
I don't care, it's flawed theology—

LAZIC
(interrupts)
Ah, you think survival demonstrates superiority—
(then)
I'll begin from the beginning. You see, I'm a sick man… a notorious scoundrel. I've known that for some time—

Pavel Kudlak

Almost immediately, Pavel picks up the wolf mask and HURLS it at the altar. KABOOM! Just missing Lazic's noggin. A thousand shattered pieces. After a beat... Lazic calmly collects the broken mask... he's deep in thought.

> LAZIC
> (continuing)
> As you've revealed—fear can take different shapes.

A momentary pause... then...

> PAVEL
> My father is dead, Mister Lazic.

Lazic's movements stop. Clearly, he's hurt by the news.

> PAVEL
> (continuing)
> How well did you know him?

Lazic glares at him—unsure; as Pavel waits.

> LAZIC
> We were lovers, Pavel. A long time ago… But you already knew that or you wouldn't have come here today.

PAVEL
Did my mother know?

Pavel studies him. Lazic hesitating.

LAZIC
I suspect she didn't.
(beat)
Men lack sufficient focus… a woman, on the other hand, is a dreamer—she's a different breed.

PAVEL
You mean she was in love.

LAZIC
She was… and with more than one man. She would not divorce him—

PAVEL
(interrupts)
What do you mean?

Lazic hesitating… then…

LAZIC
I was hired… to do a job—

Pavel Kudlak

Pavel pulls out his .45 caliber semi-automatic and points it at Lazic's body.

> PAVEL
> (interrupts)
> You pig—I should execute you now.

Lazic drops to his knees for a moment... then he rises... staring into Pavel's eyes.

> LAZIC
> Do what pleases you... I'm not pleading for my life—now that it has little meaning—

Pavel's gun points to his head.

> LAZIC
> (continuing)
> Who could have guessed your mother would be so captivating? Her voice was kind and sincere—almost angelic... I was unable to make my usual fast reply. And, for a fleeting moment, it seemed like eternity. I fancied that, and her, and changed my view of many things.
> (MORE)

LAZIC (CONT'D)
Then, imagine my shock and surprise, when a faint smile appeared... I sensed an uncertain guilt, a restless longing, and maybe a lingering shame...
(smiles)
I see now that I'm getting ahead of myself—

Pavel has brought his left hand to his pistol— readying to fire at any second.

LAZIC
(continuing)
You do not understand... come to your senses, boy. Don't you see I was hired by your father to kill your—

As Lazic speaks... Pavel takes final aim and FIRES a single fatal shot into his head. We see the bullet enter Lazic's forehead, between his eyes. The impact sends Lazic reeling backward— buckled knees, eyes and mouth wide open.

Pavel studies the corpse for a long moment. Then he holsters his gun and exits the apartment.

Pavel Kudlak

EXT. FREEWAY – DAY

We see Pavel's Jag hauling ass through freeway traffic.

In time... we see a large sign indicating the coast highway. At last, the Jag takes the exit heading to the harbor.

EXT. MARINA – DAY

Now the Jag arrives at the security gate of a prestigious yacht club. We see Pavel questioning the guard standing outside the security shack. The guard points to a luxury yacht moored not far behind his shelter. A moment later, the security gate comes up and the Jag drives through.

Pavel parks the car and sprints to the dock. FINALLY, he jumps onto the starboard bow of the fishing yacht called, "Solitary Hunter."

EXT. FISHING YACHT – DAY

We're on the aft deck of a 60-foot "Hatteras" sport fishing yacht. Jaws is relaxing next to a stacked little blonde in a yellow bikini.

Telico arrives on deck, dressed in a tight business suit.

> TELICO
> Mister Fedele, Pavel is on board.

> JAWS
> I'll take care of it. Let's cast off.

Telico nods and splits.

After a beat… Pavel stands on the aft deck.

> PAVEL
> I just had a chat with Lazic—he's not doing so great.

Jaws looks at him.

> JAWS
> And now you wanna chat with me… be my guest.

> PAVEL
> Fill in the gaps, Mister Fedele. I want the truth.

The crew of the yacht make ready to leave the marina. All dock lines are collected… finally… the "Solitary Hunter" makes out of the harbor.

Pavel Kudlak

The yacht is now cruising the coastal waters—not in any hurry. A little later... it begins to move slower. Slower yet... until it's hardly moving at all.

Jaws looks out onto the water.

JAWS
I wanna show you something.

Then... he goes into the bait bucket and... throws bloody bait and blood into the green water. Pavel watches.

JAWS
(continuing)
I have thought about this day for a long time. Waiting... wondering when it would come... what I would do. Unfortunately, answers do not always help us heal.

THEN... a light green shark with a white underbelly slowly circles the bait. It looks to be about 10 feet in length. Five-gill slits, two dorsal fins and an anal fin says that it's a tiger shark—"the man eater."

Pavel has noticed the circling shark.

PAVEL
No more fuckin games.
>(beat)
You're somehow connected to all this—

JAWS
>(interrupts)
Games… I love games. Soon, everybody goes home a winner.

Pavel unbuttons his jacket. We see his pistol in the holster.

Jaws sees the gun too.

JAWS
>(continuing)
You're in enough trouble already.

Pavel studies him.

Jaws carefully opens the transom door… he stands there, looking at Pavel for the longest… THEN… Jaws looks at the circling shark and casually JUMPS into the dangerous water.

The tiger shark immediately ATTACKS him. We hear Jaws GROAN… the water turns red and white... a considerable amount of chaos and tension. The blonde SCREAMING hysterically.

Pavel pulls out his gun and FIRES numerous shots into the tiger shark. In the end... killing the tiger.

Jaws is floating in the water—he's not dead but looks to be critically injured. Finally... Pavel, Telico and a crew member manage to pull Jaws out of the water and onto the deck.

His injuries are severe. Telico pressing a white towel against a gaping torso gash—the white mass of cotton quickly turns red.

Pavel bent over Jaws—supporting his head. Jaws looks into his eyes—there's a faint smile on his face.

> PAVEL
> You're going to be fine, Mister Fedele. Don't move; hang on.
> (to the crew)
> Get this yacht to the marina.

The yacht makes a quick turn toward the harbor. Both engines are maxed out—the yacht slicing through the waves.

> JAWS
> I'm sorry… You're my flesh and blood—I couldn't let you kill me.

Then… Jaws takes a last breath… and dies.

A surreal calm descends over Pavel. For a moment, he's catatonic. His eyes become moist… at last, his hands release Jaws. Then… gently, he grasps Telico by the collar.

> PAVEL
> He's my father… you knew… you knew.

Telico's bloody hands are on top of Pavel's grip… he just looks at him—unable to speak. A deep sadness has overtaken Telico. His lower lip is quivering.

After a beat… our view expands. An aerial view of the fishing yacht… traveling slowly… toward the marina in the distance.

FADE OUT.

THE END

About the Author

MEHMET SERDAR TEKBAŞ was born in 1953, in Istanbul, Turkey. In 1963, he settled with his family in Canada. Mehmet has studied at the University of Windsor and the University of Toronto. He enjoys nature, Russian novels, cosmology, and dabbling in the stock market. Mehmet is the author of *This is Okinawan Karate*. *Pavel Kudlak* is his debut screenplay. Contact Mehmet at mstekbas@live.ca

www.ingramcontent.com/pod-product-compliance
Lightning Source LLC
Chambersburg PA
CBHW071504040426
42444CB00008B/1495